The Holy Hand Grenade

The Holy Hand Grenade

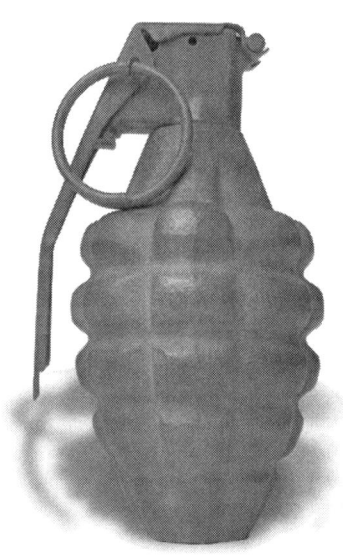

How to get
what you really
want, really!

*Dan,
Find your GIFT and
unleash you Passion.
TJ Gilroy*

THOMAS J. GILROY

WestBow
PRESS

Copyright © 2013 Thomas J. Gilroy.

All rights reserved. No part of this book may be used or reproduced by any means, graphic, electronic, or mechanical, including photocopying, recording, taping or by any information storage retrieval system without the written permission of the publisher except in the case of brief quotations embodied in critical articles and reviews.

WestBow Press books may be ordered through booksellers or by contacting:

WestBow Press
A Division of Thomas Nelson
1663 Liberty Drive
Bloomington, IN 47403
www.westbowpress.com
1-(866) 928-1240

Because of the dynamic nature of the Internet, any web addresses or links contained in this book may have changed since publication and may no longer be valid. The views expressed in this work are solely those of the author and do not necessarily reflect the views of the publisher, and the publisher hereby disclaims any responsibility for them.

Any people depicted in stock imagery provided by Thinkstock are models, and such images are being used for illustrative purposes only.

Certain stock imagery © Thinkstock.

Edited by Chris Safford.

ISBN: 978-1-4497-8589-5 (sc)
ISBN: 978-1-4497-8588-8 (hc)
ISBN: 978-1-4497-859-01 (e)

Library of Congress Control Number: 2013903100

Printed in the United States of America

WestBow Press rev. date: 8/30/2013

Table of Contents

Introduction. ix

Foundation

Chapter 1	The Killer Rabbit and the Bridge of Death	3
Chapter 2	Asking Questions	9
Chapter 3	The Socratic Method	13
Chapter 4	Assumptions	17

The First Question

Chapter 5	Back to the Bridge of Death.	25
Chapter 6	Who am I, Really?	29
Chapter 7	Personality	33
Chapter 8	Who's Your Daddy?	45
Chapter 9	How You Give and Receive Love	55
Chapter 10	How You Think.	61
Chapter 11	Confidence	69

The Second Question

Chapter 12	The Second Question	75
Chapter 13	Security versus Freedom.	81
Chapter 14	Talent	85
Chapter 15	Comparison.	93
Chapter 16	Developing Your Gift	99
Chapter 17	Resistance.	101

The Third Question

Chapter 18	The Third Question	115
Chapter 19	Eleven Reasons Why People Do Not Know Their Burning Desires	121
Chapter 20	Passion	131
Chapter 21	Ask, Seek, Knock	141
Chapter 22	Free Will	145
Chapter 23	More than Enough	149
Chapter 24	Let's Get Real	153
Chapter 25	Mentorship	157
Chapter 26	How and Where Do You Fit In?	161
Chapter 27	Vision	165
Chapter 28	Comparison, Part 2	171
Chapter 29	Purpose	173
Chapter 30	Competition versus Creativity	177

Application

Chapter 31	I.C.I.—Applying your gift	183
Chapter 32	Ambush	187
Chapter 33	Examples	191
Chapter 34	Just Imagine	205
Chapter 35	Epilogue	209
Recommended Reading		*211*
About the Author		*213*

Introduction

> ***Quest:***
> *an act or instance of seeking, pursuing or searching,*
> *sometimes involving an adventurous journey*

Imagine tonight, as you sleep, that God zaps you with a lightning bolt, and when you awake, you are living the perfect life. You get to wake up every morning from now on and do exactly what you were meant to do. You feel fulfilled and appreciated. You have no more concerns about having to impress anyone, and money no longer worries you. You are operating on all cylinders, and you feel full of life. The lack of stress in your life has a direct impact on your health, and you feel better than you have for years. Wouldn't that be great?

Believe it or not, that is exactly what I expected to happen to me. So I waited for a lightning bolt, and I waited, and I waited.

There might be someone out there who actually did get hit by lightning and woke up to the perfect life, but I don't recommend waiting for it to happen to you. There is a much better way that can work for almost everyone. I am not a natural conversationalist, and writing a book about anything seemed like one of the least likely things I would ever do. The reason I went through the ordeal of writing is that I found my passion, and once I found mine, it seemed as if everyone I spoke to told me they wished they could find theirs. So, in a way, I wrote *The Holy Hand Grenade* out of a sense of obligation to help others find what I found.

My favorite conversation starter—I actually need a pre-planned starter because I don't normally talk to people I don't know—is to ask about what they do. Since most people don't like what they do or are biding their time until they discover their true passions, that question usually turns into a second question about what they really want to do. About eighty percent of the time, a person's response to this question is "I don't know" or "I wish I knew."

That was my first clue that the majority of people don't know what they want, aren't passionate about what they are currently doing and don't know where to start looking. They are waiting to get struck by lightning. Something inside me said that wasn't right, and a mission to fix it started to grow.

I found a way to uncover my own real desires, and found what worked for me works for almost everyone. However, there are a few things that can deter someone from finding his or her passion.

Trust

The world seems to get busier and more complicated every year. As technology increases, so does competition for your attention. Television competes with the Internet for viewers. Smart-phones compete with tablets for media usage. Billboards, radio, Facebook, Twitter, Google, television, wireless devices, and magazines compete to market products for your consideration. All this competition for your attention makes it difficult to decide who to trust for reliable information you need when making decisions.

In this "Information Age," trust has also been shaken by institutions that were formerly trustworthy. Banks were once trusted to protect our money. The U.S. Securities and Exchange Commission was once trusted to protect our investments. Government was once trusted to do the right thing for the people it represents. The Church was once trusted to be ethical and moral. The family was once trusted to teach values and be a safe haven for its members. Marriage was once trusted to be an institution of commitment between men and women who loved each other. All of these institutions have come under attack and are not as trustworthy as they once were or should be.

Recognizing that trust is an issue, I ask you to keep an open mind as you read the following pages. I am asking you to take a break from all of the noise of the world and to trust in—and think for—yourself. Two areas that are difficult for people to think about for themselves are religion and politics. Whether we want to admit it or not, our opinions about religion and politics are largely formed before we are old enough to reason for ourselves. Overcoming preconceptions in these two areas can be difficult, but this is necessary in getting the answers you deserve.

Religion

In the movie *Kingdom of Heaven*[1], there is a powerful scene that helps set the foundation for this book you are reading. The movie begins in medieval Europe at the time of the first crusade, an unforgiving time when kings and bishops reigned supremely. Balian (played by Orlando Bloom) is the village blacksmith and an illegitimate son of Godfrey, the baron of Ibelin. Through a series of events, Balian becomes the new baron of Ibelin in the Holy Land near Jerusalem.

Having inherited his father's land, title, and knighthood, Balian arrives in Jerusalem. Yet, he is not his father, and he struggles trying to understand his own identity. He undertook the journey from France to Jerusalem to seek forgiveness for the heavy burden of sin and guilt he carries. His sins include his illegitimate birth, his wife's suicide following the death of their child, and the small matter of his killing of a local priest in his native France. Saying that he was a troubled young man would be an understatement.

In the scene, he speaks with a Hospitaller, which was a sort of combination priest/knight/doctor. The Hospitaller is a good friend of Balian's father and has become a mentor to Balian. The scene unfolds as follows:

Hospitaller: How find you Jerusalem?

Balian: God does not speak to me, not even on the hill where Christ died…I am outside God's grace.

---

1   *The Kingdom of Heaven*, 2005, Twentieth Century Fox

Hospitaller: I have not heard that.

Balian: It seems I have lost my religion.

Hospitaller: I put no stock in religion. By the word *religion*, I've seen the lunacy of fanatics of every denomination be called the "will of God." Holiness is in right action and courage on behalf of those who cannot defend themselves…And "goodness," what God desires, is here (he points to Balian's head) and here (he points to Balian's heart)…and what you decide to do every day, you will be a good man or not.

I think that scene is so powerful because it implies that even one thousand years ago, religion (man-made denominations, doctrines, rituals, and creeds as opposed to a relationship with God) had a hand in confusing people. Balian went to Jerusalem seeking forgiveness and entry into a heaven that was promised by religion. He found in Jerusalem an apparent contradiction between what was sanctioned by religion and what he knew to be right. Since he did not find his conscience eased for his deeds in France, he questioned what he believed. Many people today have lost their "religion," and often for good reasons. The conversation with Balian and the Hospitaller is fictitious, but it hits close to the mark for a large number of Americans today. Balian was seeking forgiveness and a purpose for his life. The Hospitaller advised him that being right with God had to do with how he thought and what he did, rather than about a set of rules. Balian followed the Hospitaller's advice and ended up doing something truly great. By following his conscience and doing what he knew was right, he saved the city of Jerusalem from annihilation at the hands of a Moslem army.

The Holy Hand Grenade addresses three questions you will need to answer in order to fulfill your quest. To answer the three questions, you do not need religion. In fact, having an unquestioned religion could actually prevent you from finding the answers you richly deserve.

However, I cannot tell you the truth without entering God into the equation. It is interesting that the meaning of "truth" came up during the process of writing this book. Many people apparently have different concepts of the meaning of the word. In order for something to be true, it has to always be true. If something is the truth on occasion, but not always, then it is not the truth – it is, more or less, an opinion. If someone peddles a "truth" that is really an opinion, there is more than likely an ulterior motive behind his effort. If there is an ulterior motive behind what is perceived to be the truth, then how can it really be trusted? Being able to discern the truth from an opinion—or, worse yet, a deception—has been the source of much of today's skepticism. This has often been the case with organized religions.

I bring this up at the beginning of this book because the lack of trust that is prevalent in our country could have its origins in this thought: people may not know what "the truth" is. This problem is not a new issue. In fact, it is the same issue Pilate presented to Jesus prior to Jesus' crucifixion. In a moment when he seemed perplexed, Pilate asked, "What is truth?[2]" The truth was a relative term even 2000 years ago, and Pilate seemingly did not know what truth was and what fiction was. Without God, you cannot know the truth, and you will be subject to all sorts of opinions as a result. Perhaps you were raised to believe a certain way about God, but do you really know God personally? If not, how do you know if what you were taught is the truth? Part of the lack of trust in the world can be attributed to competing religions, each espousing "the truth." I suggest you find the truth for yourself, and don't accept someone else's opinion as a substitute. I think that is the message the Hospitaller wished to convey to Balian.

Equipped with the truth, you will be able to answer the three questions posed in this book. The U.S. Declaration of Independence clearly states, "We hold these truths to be self-evident, that all men are created equal, that they are endowed by their Creator with certain unalienable rights, that among these are life, liberty and the pursuit of happiness."

America was founded on a belief in God, not on a belief in religion. So, if you have lost your religion, or you never had one to begin with, the following pages should make sense to you. But—and there's a big BUT—if you don't believe in the Creator, don't read this book. It won't help you.

Throughout the following pages, you will note quotes and references from the Bible. Regardless of how spiritual you are, or whether you come from a "religious" background or not, the Bible has withstood the test of time as a source of knowledge and truth, so I feel it is entirely appropriate to quote from the Bible in order to answer life's most challenging questions.

---

2   *The Holy Bible*, John 18:38

I have quoted and referenced the "New American Standard Version" of the Bible in this book. There are many awesome versions and translations of the Bible; it is not my intent to recommend one over another.

Politics

Another source of mistrust in America today is our political system. There seem to be two political schools of thought: one claims to be liberal and the other conservative. If you are liberal, then the word "conservative" is like a curse word. If you are conservative, the word "liberal" almost equates to being un-American. As I see it, neither camp is entirely correct; and this battle has been raging since John Adams and Thomas Jefferson went at it.

Liberals feel they should take care of the masses, because the masses can't take care of themselves. For a variety of reasons, liberals think they have been blessed with more wealth, intelligence or fortune than have other Americans. They seem to feel they have a responsibility to spread that blessing to those less fortunate. That was John Adams' stance.

Conservatives think the Constitution and the American way of life provide (or should provide) an equal opportunity for all Americans to obtain as much or as little as they want. Conservatives seem to think that handing unearned money or other unearned blessings to people will only hurt them in the long run by taking away their incentives to better themselves. Conservatives believe the American people are smart enough to figure things out. Conservatives don't want an elite intelligentsia doing their thinking for them.

From my perspective, both political sides are lacking and not worthy of our trust. I feel that rather than arguing over politics, religion or any other ideology, we each should strive to reach our own potential, and help others do the same. That is the focus of *The Holy Hand Grenade*. As the Hospitaller told Balian, if you use your mind and your heart, you will be able to correctly discern "the truth," and knowing the truth will set you free.

Good reading!

PART I

Foundation

Chapter 1

The Killer Rabbit and the Bridge of Death

Before I get started, I recommend you read the introduction, if you haven't already. It could save you heartburn, later.

The summer between my high school graduation and my freshman year in college, I worked up the courage to ask my high school heartthrob, Ann, on a date. She was very attractive and very smart, and her dad was a Marine Corps pilot, which was exactly what I wanted to be. Ann had it all.

Some of my friends told me about a funny movie that had just come out. Ann and I barely knew each other, so I figured a funny movie would be just the ticket to break the ice. I asked Ann if she wanted to see the movie with me. To my utter amazement, she said yes.

We bought popcorn and Cokes and headed into the theater. As the movie started, I had a grave feeling I had made a mistake. Normally, opening credits for movies are ignored (no one pays attention to the credits), but not this time. There were weird comments about a majestic moose (comments made in pigeon-English/Swedish), and then the editor apologized for the credits being absurd and told the audience that those responsible had been sacked. Just as we thought things were going back to normal, this announcement appeared on the screen: "*The directors of the firm hired to continue the credits after the other people had been sacked, wish it to be known that they have just been sacked. The credits have been completed in an entirely different style at great expense and at the last minute.*

Executive Producer

JOHN GOLDSTONE & 'RALPH' The Wonder Llama."

Then the credits morphed into a Mexican music theme and discussions about llamas.

People in the audience were laughing, and the movie hadn't even started. Ann sat quiet and straight-faced, without as much as a giggle. My palms were soaked, and it wasn't from holding my Coke! I knew I lost Ann five minutes into the movie, around the point King Arthur chopped off the Black Knight's arm. Obviously fake blood was melodramatically squirting from where the Black Knight's arm had been. The Black Knight looked at King Arthur and said defiantly, "It's only a flesh wound!" I laughed out loud. (For those of you who have never seen it, I'm talking about the cult classic, *Monty Python's King Arthur and the Holy Grail*[3].) Ann looked at me as if I were the weirdest guy she'd ever met. To her credit, she lasted through the movie, but there was no conversation on the way home.

I want you to know I was persistent. After a disastrous first date with Ann, I went back for more—Ann and I were done, but I went back to see the movie over and over.

I probably saw Monty Python at least twenty more times, and it's amazing how much better the movie got when I watched it with a bunch of rowdy guys and had a few beers under my belt. To this day, I'm amazed at how many people I meet who can quote lines from that movie. During a business advisory board meeting I held, a former Navy Seal captain quoted a scene from the movie. He took me completely by surprise, but everyone in the meeting knew exactly what he was talking about. Even my sister and her second-year-college daughter were quoting Monty Python

---

3 *Month Python and the Holy Grail*, 1975, Almi Cinema 5

at a recent dinner we had together. So, I discovered there are a few women who think that movie is really funny. (My wife is not one of them: and no, her name is not Ann).

I shared this disastrous memory from my youth with you for a good reason. Believe it or not, a scene in that movie helped me set the outline for this book, and another scene helped me to find the right title.

During the Monty Python version of King Arthur's quest for the Holy Grail, Arthur and his knights had to pass through a cave guarded by a fierce, terrible beast. The terrifying creature made many a brave knight soil his armor. After two valiant attempts to kill the beast, Arthur and his men retreated, found cover behind some rocks, and consulted a "book of armaments" for a weapon to dispose of the dreaded creature. The weapon of choice needed to kill the beast was the "Holy Hand Grenade of Antioch." When King Arthur pulled the pin on the Holy Hand Grenade and lobbed it at the beast, sure enough, the beast was destroyed, and they continued on their quest. The scene was quite funny, especially after I realized the horrible and terrifying beast was a white bunny rabbit.

For the purposes of this book, the Holy Hand Grenade scene is a metaphor. The horrible beast guarded a place the king and his knights had to pass through to continue their journey. In other words, the creature was a PEST that had to be dealt with. As you will discover in chapter 19, "PEST" is an acronym. It stands for **P**eople, **E**motions, **S**urvival and **T**hinking. The PEST created so much fear that most would-be seekers turned back and didn't try to continue. Others tried, as did King Arthur and his knights, to conquer their fears and overcome the PEST with only their own resources, namely their courage and swords. The cave's entrance was littered with the bones of those foolish enough to try to conquer the beast in their own strength. In this metaphor, Arthur knew three things.

1. He wasn't going to let a PEST, or his fear of that PEST, stop him from getting what he wanted.
2. He was smart enough not to let his pride or arrogance (about his own strength) get him killed.
3. He realized he needed additional help (in the form of a Holy Hand Grenade) to continue his quest.

The point is this: Once you decide to begin the quest for what you want most, you will face obstacles. Probably the biggest obstacle you face will be some kind of fear, rather than a ferocious killer rabbit. Some obstacles you can—and should—conquer in your own strength. But sooner or later, you are going to run into an obstacle or fear that you can't defeat by yourself. Then you will have the same choices as King Arthur had: You can run away; you can die trying; or you can get help. If you are seeking something great from your life, you will eventually realize the need for some greater firepower. Whether you call it having another tool in your chest, or another arrow in your quiver, or a Holy Hand Grenade, you'll need something bigger than yourself to get whatever you seek.

Further on in Monty Python's version of King Arthur's travels, Arthur and a handful of his knights approached the Bridge of Death. If they could cross that bridge, they believed they would find the Holy Grail. In order to pass over the bridge, they first had to contend with a horrible old man named "The Bridge Keeper."

If Arthur and his knights could answer the Bridge Keeper's questions, he would allow them to cross the bridge, but if they failed to answer all three questions correctly, they would die by being thrown into a deep gorge. The first knight answered his questions with no problem. The second knight wasn't so lucky. After stumbling on the third question (about his favorite color), he was tossed into the gorge. When King Arthur's turn came to answer the Bridge Keeper, the scene went something like this:

Bridge Keeper: Who would cross the Bridge of Death must answer me these questions three, ere the other side he see. What is your name?

Arthur: Arthur, King of the Britons.

Bridge Keeper: What is your quest?

Arthur: To seek the Holy Grail.

Bridge Keeper: What is the airspeed velocity of an un-laden swallow?

Arthur: An African or European Swallow?

Bridge Keeper: I don't know that…ooooooh…. (The Bridge Keeper himself was flung to his death in the deep gorge.)

Then, Sir Galahad asked King Arthur, as they crossed over the Bridge of Death, "How do you know so much about swallows?"

Arthur: You have to know these things when you are king.

I rented the movie, again, to make sure I had correctly written the Killer Rabbit and Bridge of Death scenes. Those scenes weren't quite as funny as they were when I viewed them nearly twenty times with my beer-drinking friends. By watching the movie, again, I did, however, decide on my book's title: *The Holy Hand Grenade, How to get what you really want, REALLY!*

This book is based on three very significant questions. (No, not the ones King Arthur had to answer). Like Arthur and his knights, you have to correctly answer some of life's questions if you want to find your "Holy Grail." While you most likely will not be thrown into a deep gorge to your death if you don't answer the questions posed in this book (although, you might want to bone up on your knowledge of African and European swallow airspeed velocity, just in case), you will be more or less a zombie in life (another movie reference). In other words, without answering these three questions, you will never be really alive or reach the greatness inside of you. In fact, you may not even start the quest to find what you really want if you cannot answer these questions.

The third question was the one that sent some of King Arthur's knights to their deaths. So, while the first two questions were important, the third question tripped up many of the knights. I realize it's a bit of a stretch to find significance in a silly movie, but as Saint James said, "You have not, because you ask not[4]." So, asking questions is a key to getting what you really want.

---

4 *The Holy Bible*, James 4:2

CHAPTER 2

Asking Questions

I REMEMBER, AS IF IT WAS yesterday, the day I started asking the right questions.

It was December 1987. I was lying on my bunk on the USS Okinawa, trying to get some sleep before our next mission. I served as a captain in the Marine Corps and as a Cobra helicopter pilot on a big grey boat in the middle of the Persian Gulf. Iran and Iraq were busy trying to kill each other in a messy war, and we were there to protect our oil tankers from being sunk by the Iranians.

Our preparation for going to the Persian Gulf and the possibility of going into combat had been very exciting. Preparing for a real mission (as opposed to regular training missions) was quite intense. We also had 300 infantry Marines on board. All of them were itching for action.

As a Captain on my second flying tour, I was at the pinnacle of my career as a Marine officer. I was still a junior officer but had eight years of experience, and the "experts" said that particular time in a Marine officer's career was "where it was at." But, it didn't feel that way.

Though Christmas was just around the corner, no one on the ship felt in a holiday mood. Tossing and turning in my bunk, I could think only about how much I missed my new wife. We had married the previous January and being in the Persian Gulf in December meant I was missing our first Christmas and our first anniversary. I was fully aware "this" was what I signed up for, and if my squadron had been engaged in something more important than protecting oil tankers, I might have felt better about my place of duty and missing my anniversary.

I vividly recall the night in the Persian Gulf when asking the right questions set me on the right course. Lying on my bunk, I was awake and staring up at the overhead (ships don't have "ceilings"; they have "overheads"). I recall my stateroom was illuminated by the dim red light of a warship at night, and that a deep sense of emptiness suddenly came over me. It was as if I awoke to the reality that I wasn't doing what I was meant to do with my life, and at that moment I knew there had to be more. I remember asking God, out loud, "Is this it? Is this what I am supposed to do for the rest of my life?"

Maybe your moment was the same; maybe it was different; or maybe you haven't had your moment, yet. Still, most people eventually ask this question: "Is this it?"

Being a Marine captain and pilot was what I had wanted since I was a child. I was six years old when my dad served as the Sergeant Major of the Marine Barracks at Roosevelt Roads, Puerto Rico. One day, he took me down to the flight line on the base and somehow got a pilot to let me sit in the cockpit of a Marine A-4 Skyhawk jet. Pilots sometimes flew to Puerto Rico from the U.S. mainland on "training flights." More often than not, those training flights were booze runs, because they could buy cases of alcohol, without paying taxes, and carry them back to their U.S. bases.

As a six-year-old kid sitting in the cockpit of a really cool jet, I was in heaven. I was so small that I couldn't see over the instrument panel. When the pilot put his helmet on me, it was so big that when I turned my head, the helmet stayed still while my head rotated in it. I couldn't see a thing, but that didn't matter. I thought the experience was great! I visualized being a Marine pilot from that point until it became a reality. But that night, while lying on a bunk on the USS Okinawa I came to the sudden realization that being a career Marine wasn't "it" for me.

The problem was that I had no idea what "it" was. The idea of being a Marine pilot was probably more of a romantic notion based on the heroic stories I grew up with rather than on the realities of the profession. My father, a World War II and Korean War Veteran who was highly respected by his peers and his family, was my hero. The realities of the not-so-romantic profession, the boredom of life on a ship, and being separated from the wife I loved made me question whether I really wanted to continue as a pilot for the rest of my life. There had to be more. To make matters worse, no one I knew had figured "it" out for themselves, either. I asked my other pilot buddies about their decisions to stay in the Marine Corps. I sought advice from my senior officers and even asked the Marine colonel who was in charge of all the Marines on the ship how he made his career choice. Everyone seemed to be just going with the flow, not really making any decisions at all. Once I asked the right question, I became aware of how many people were just going from day to day, without real hope of realizing any greatness in their lives.

So the hunt was on. The more questions I asked about what people wanted to do with their lives, the more I realized that people I looked up to were in the same predicament I was. The really scary part was how many of them were resigned to not getting any answers.

I began asking myself why they weren't seeking answers. At the same time, my wife, Mary, was going through some of the same turmoil with her Navy career. We both decided to take our disillusions and turn them into actions. Even though we enjoyed our military careers, we knew it was time to find what we were really supposed to do with our lives. Neither of us knew what that was.

We just knew we weren't going to find it in the military. So, we resigned our commissions and ventured into the business world in search of "it." Shortly after resigning from the Marine Corps, I heard this quote: "The mass of men lead lives of quiet desperation." I didn't know who said that or the circumstances surrounding that quote, but those words nailed what I observed in myself and in most people I knew. About two years ago, I discovered this second part of that quote: "What is called resignation is confirmed desperation." Both sentences making up that quotation were written by Henry David Thoreau in the 1860s. I found Thoreau's quote reassuring in that I was not the only one who thought those thoughts. On the other hand, the quote was disconcerting in that so few people seemed to have answers that could make a difference. The quiet desperation I started to see all around me became my reason to ask more questions.

> The mass of men lead lives of quiet desperation. What is called resignation is confirmed desperation.
>
> Henry David Thoreau

Chapter 3

The Socratic Method

When I returned from the Persian Gulf, even though I was sure the Marine Corps was not "it" for me, I did not immediately leave. I served with the marines for two more years before I finally made the leap into the "real world." Ever hear about the three cats? Question: If three cats are sitting on a fence, and two of them decide to get off, how many cats will be left? Answer: Three. Deciding and doing are not the same things. Even though I had decided to make a change in my life, it took a while for me to summon the courage to actually do it.

It was my good fortune that, as Mary and I were preparing to leave the military, we were introduced to the Amway business. I'll bet some of you are wincing at that statement. Actually, my overall experience in Amway was pretty good. We achieved what is called the Ruby level, and several great things came from the time we spent in that type of business. Robert Kiyosaki, author of *Rich Dad, Poor Dad*[5] and several other good books, recommends that people wanting to become entrepreneurs begin by joining a good network marketing business. Working in network marketing is a

---

5   *Rich Dad Poor Dad*, Robert Kiyosaki

good way to get over a fear of rejection, and to acquire some business skills with little or no risk. That is exactly what happened for me.

The greatest benefit I gained from my Amway experience was the beginning of a mentor relationship with a multimillionaire named Jack, who I call my "Rich Dad." Kiyosaki based an entire business educational system on the mentor relationship he had with his "Rich Dad," his best friend's father. His "Poor Dad" was his real father. Though he loved his father and respected him greatly, his Rich Dad had the knowledge and experience Kiyosaki was really seeking. My situation was similar. My real dad was an awesome father. In fact, by today's standards, he was a model of fatherhood. He was a World War II career Marine who retired as a First Sergeant and was selected for Sergeant Major. However, dad knew little about business or how to pursue his passion. (More on that later.) Dad came from an Irish-Catholic background; his name was John. For whatever reason, Irish-Catholics named John are often given the nickname Jack. My "Rich Dad" (my business mentor) is as strong in character and demeanor as my father was; his name is also Jack. He had served as an Army Sergeant First Class. I didn't let inter-service rivalry (he had served in the Army; I had served in the Marine Corps) influence too much my opinion of him. I think the fact that he never had to think much about money did the trick.

From the outset of our relationship, Jack never told me what to do. He asked probing questions to get me thinking and then recommended articles or books to read. He usually determined if I read what he recommended by listening to questions I asked later. I began to figure out that the quality of the mentorship I received was in large part reliant on the quality of the questions I asked. By asking the right questions, I gave Jack permission to reveal the next door I should walk through. I guess you could say he guided me to self-revelation. He still does that to this day. The old adage "When the student is ready, the teacher appears" has proven true for me. I think Jack figured that people hate being told what to do, so the best way for them to learn is through self-discovery. The self-discovery process is a sort of quest that involves seeking. If you haven't already noticed, the word "question" is based on the word "quest." Asking questions involves seeking something.

This method of teaching, learning, and mentorship is sometimes referred to as the Socratic method. It is attributed to Socrates and goes back to at least 400 B.C. The Socratic method is still used by many law schools. If you watch a TV show that involves a courtroom scene, notice that asking questions of a witness is the process of examination. The main points of the Socratic method of learning are twofold. First, asking questions is extremely important in uncovering the truth. (Part of that truth is finding out what "it" is that you want to pursue in life.) Second, just asking questions is not enough. Questions have to be the right questions. In order to ask the right questions, almost all of us need mentors. It is not enough to just "have" a mentor. You need the "right" mentor, as we will discuss in more detail in Chapter 25.

Chapter 4

Assumptions

Asking the right questions begins with checking your assumptions. Whenever you plan a trip, you need to know at least two things: where you are going to start from, and where you want to go. If you begin your journey from point A, but point A is not really where you think it is, then your journey will not take you where you want to go. For example, let's say you are going on a trip from Columbus, Georgia to Washington, D.C., and you are piloting your own plane. You plug the information for your flight into a computer that gives you your flight plan, and off you go. The plan says you should fly a heading of 095 for 300 miles. You know your airspeed will be 150 miles an hour, so you should be there in two hours. About an hour and fifteen minutes into the flight, you find yourself over the Atlantic Ocean. Something is seriously wrong! You notice there is a city down there, but it is not Washington, D.C. You decide to fly a little lower, so you can read the name on a water tower. The letters on that tower spell "Savannah." How the !*@# did that happen? You take a good look at the flight plan you received from the computer. You immediately see the problem. The starting point you put into the flight plan was Columbus, but it was Columbus, Ohio, not Columbus,

Georgia. No matter how well you follow your flight plan, you will never end up in Washington, D.C.

The flight plan example is an unrealistic scenario, but it gets the point across. Assuming you know where you want to go (which may also be a false assumption), if you don't start from where you really are, not where you think or hope you are, you will never get there. You can take this even farther. If you don't know where you are going, you won't get there either. Many times, we assume we know where we are going and assume we are on course, but the truth is far different.

Prior to my revelation on board the USS Okinawa, I thought I knew where I wanted to go and how to get there. I came to my senses in the middle of the Persian Gulf. When you come to your senses, you can correct your travel plan and get back on track. Many people, upon discovering they are on the wrong path, think they have invested too heavily into where they are, and rather than making corrections, they continue on the wrong path. If you have a job that pays bills and gives you some sense of accomplishment, but in your heart you know you were meant to do something else, you may find it too easy to stay where you are. You feel as if you are a prisoner, but the prison is too nice to leave in order to pursue the freedom you yearn for. The assumption is this: you may not get your greatest desire because what you have now may be good enough. This is where "good" is the enemy of "great", and where assumptions can be fatal to your dreams and desires. The good news is that "All things come together for good, for those who love God and are called according to His purpose[6]", as St Paul says. But even in this passage of scripture, there is the assumption that one loves God and is called according to His purpose.

As I write this, our U.S. Congress is locked in a stalemate over what to do about our country's debt. Most of the country cannot understand why the Republicans and the Democrats can't get their act together and get anything productive accomplished. I say it has to do with assumptions. If we assume the members of congress all think the same and have the best interest of the United States at heart, then we assume incorrectly. The beliefs and ideals of the members of congress are not

---

6 *The Holy Bible*, Romans 8:28

even remotely the same, even within their own parties. Their agendas are also very different. Some have very noble agendas, and others are purely self-serving. I'll let you decide which is which. I do, however, find it amusing that the opposite of pro is con, so it follows that the opposite of progress is congress.

I used to think everyone thought like I do, and what was important to me was naturally important to them. That was a big mistake! I came to find out—the hard way I might add—that our personalities predispose us to thinking in certain ways. Once you realize this fact, it becomes much easier to deal with people. Until you realize this fact, some personalities seem like they are from a different planet.

Have you ever met a person who is always the life of the party? I have a friend who is a great salesman. He is loud, funny, energetic and charismatic. Do you know the type? You can't help liking the guy. He also has the attention span of a gnat, and is not at all good with details. To him, not knowing the facts is just another opportunity to make up a good story. The amazing thing is he gets away with it. My personality wants to know the facts and what the other person is looking for; I want to get right to the bottom line. I used to assume that people such as my friend were careless and inconsiderate. That is largely because of how I saw things. When I ran into people who were not as interested in facts as I was, they all thought my friend was great. I thought he was nuts. That's because I assumed people thought like I did. My friend probably thought I was a stick-in-the mud, and he may have figured other people thought I was, too. If he did, it was because he assumed everyone thought like he did.

I had to learn this with Mary, my wife, as well. Not only do we have different personalities, but there are differences in the way men and women think. Without opening up a Pandora's box, there are tons of books written about how differently men and women think. The best-known book on this subject is probably *Men are from Mars and Women are from Venus*[7]. The difference in the way men and women think has changed the face of politics, the military, the work place and sports, and the list could go on and on. Most people know this by now. What they don't realize is how the differences between men and women are exacerbated by the difference in

---

7   *Men are From Mars, Women are From Venus*, John Gray

personality types. So, if you think what is important to you is the same thing that is important to the person next to you, you should check your assumption. If you think they think the same way you do, again, you should check your assumption.

There are differences in generations as well. As a baby boomer, I had real issues with "net-geners" (those that grew up with the Internet) or "millennials" (those who graduated from high school in 2000 or thereafter), or "generation Y" (another name for the same generation, and following the X generation). After reading a very interesting *USA Today* article a couple of years ago about the millennial generation, I decided to ask some questions of the twenty-somethings at my office. I asked them what they meant by asking me "Why?" when I told them to do something. My baby boomer thought process, along with my Marine Corps background, took it as a direct challenge to my authority when someone asked me "Why?" when I told him or her to do something. I assumed they were being insubordinate. The answer the millennials gave me was very revealing and showed me how far off base I was. Every one of them said they asked "Why?" in order to get a better understanding of what was wanted, so they could do a better job the first time, rather than having to repeat their work until they got it right. Millennials are used to having a lot of information available in order to complete a project. They are also used to working in groups and pooling resources to accomplish tasks. So asking "Why?" was their way of getting as full an understanding of what was required as possible, so they could do a good job.

The office conversation became loud and very excited. I was excited to find out what they really thought, and they were excited to have a baby boomer even bother to ask. It got so raucous that the CEO (another baby boomer) came out of his office to join the conversation. He overheard almost everything that was said, and chimed in that he had the same issue with his teenage kids. We all, both the baby boomers and the millennials, learned we had assumed some things incorrectly. I still don't like being asked "Why?" by millennials, but now I know what they mean, and I don't take offense.

Assumptions can run rampant on the Internet as well. Most of the time that's because we assume what is written is true. The truth can be something different, altogether. I remember seeing a website photo of a military diver on a rope ladder, hanging out of a helicopter in San Francisco Bay. Beneath him was a huge great white shark leaping out of the water. It looked as if the shark was trying to eat him off of the ladder. It was an awesome photo. The caption and the story that went with it completed the photo to make it appear spectacular and horrifying. I learned days later that the whole thing was a prank and had been Photo-shopped. There are conspiracy theories, allegations about people and companies, news reports and "expert accounts" of all kinds on the internet, in fact, that have no basis of truth at all. Determining fact from fiction can be a real task, but if you don't think for yourself and do some fact-checking of your own, you can make bad choices based on faulty assumptions.

Ask yourself these questions. What do you assume about Global Warming? What do you assume about evolution? What about your religion? What about how you decide what is right and what is wrong? Who told you? Do you really know if they told the truth, or did you just assume they knew what they were talking about? In fact, what is true? What is truth? As previously mentioned, when Jesus stood before Pilate to be tried for insurrection, he told Pilate that he came to testify to the truth. Pilate answered him with a strange question: "What is truth?" I don't think Pilate was trying to be a smart aleck. I think he was asking a profound question that really perplexed his soul. What is truth? Do you know, or are you making an assumption?

Checking your assumptions is an exercise you should go through whenever you need to make an important decision. After a while it can become a habit, but at first, you will probably have to do it on purpose. Many assumptions are actually the result of allowing someone else to do your thinking for you. This cannot be allowed. You have the gift, and the right, to be able to think for yourself. Sadly, very few people exercise that right. Are your assumptions based on facts or opinions? Sometimes, you will not have all the facts, but if checking your assumptions has become a habit of yours, then your intuition will often be just as good as a fact, mostly because it is yours. On the other hand, if your assumptions are based on the opinions of others, then you cannot blame anyone but yourself when your decisions don't work out.

One last thought on assumptions: Don't let someone else's hypocrisy keep you from the truth. Don't let the poor assumptions and bad decisions of your spouse, your parents, your religion, your government, or anyone else keep you from crossing over the Bridge of Death. When you **know** the truth, it really will set you free.

Now for the first question.

Part II

The First Question

Chapter 5

Back to the Bridge of Death

When King Arthur approached the Bridge of Death, the first question the Bridge Keeper asked him was "What is your name?" His answer was actually profound. Arthur didn't just say "Arthur." He said, "I am Arthur, king of the Britons." His answer wasn't just his name but a complete answer as to who he was. Arthur thought of himself as the king of his people. This gave him self-worth and a sense of purpose. Again, it is silly to try to draw any deep conclusions from a movie as goofy as *Monty Python and the Holy Grail*, but in this case, it works.

In my seminars, I start by asking each person to take out a sheet of paper and a pen. I ask each participant to fill in the following statement:

I am **(you fill in the blank)**   .

I give group participants 15 seconds to fill in their answers.

You try it.

Did you finish the statement in 15 seconds, or did you have to think about it longer? Did your "I am" statement describe your job or title? Did it describe your position in a family? Is that the real you? If you can't state who you are with confidence, and quickly, then there is a very real probability you don't know the answer. Wouldn't you agree this is something you should know?

Here is another question. Was your response an assumption? One of the biggest assumptions most of us make has to do with who we really are. Many people think they are who other people tell them they are. Maybe their assumptions are based on the influence of their parents, siblings, teachers, friends, or peers. If the influence was good, then the assumption may be good. But most often, the people we love the most tell us who we are not. How many times have you heard someone whose opinion you valued tell you "You can't do that" or "Who do you think you are?" How much have these comments influenced your opinion of yourself? If an influence you received took place before you were old enough to reason for yourself, I can tell you that it had a very profound influence. Psychologists argue about the exact age, but from the time you were born until you were about five or six years old, just about everything you were told by your parents and the authorities in your life went straight into your mind, completely unfiltered. So, do you really know who you are?

The question "Who am I, really?" is the first of the three questions. This is not a new question. In the Sixth Century B.C., Sun Tzu wrote *The Art of War*[8]. In it he said this:

"If you know others and know yourself, you will not be imperiled in a hundred battles; if you do not know others but know yourself, you will win one and lose one; if you do not know others and do not know yourself, you will be imperiled in every single battle."

In 400 B.C., Socrates coined the phrase *"Know Thyself."* Shakespeare said, "This above all: to thine own self be true...."[9] However, the most important reference to answering this question comes from the Gospel. Jesus said that the entire Gospel was based on two commandments, the second of which is "Love your neighbor as yourself.[10]" You cannot love your neighbor until you love yourself, and you cannot love what you do not know.

---

8   *The Art of War*, Sun Tsu

9   *Hamlet*, Act 1, scene 3, William Shakespeare

10 *The Holy Bible*, Matthew 22:37-40

Today's challenge of really knowing who you are is the result of how complex the world has become. In an age where technology doubles every two years, and where there is more change reported in the Sunday edition of any newspaper than during the entire eighteenth century, keeping up can be difficult. We have more influences on us now, than at any time in history. This generation has been marketed to through radio, television, mobile phones, magazines, newspapers, the Internet, Facebook, Twitter and a whole host of new and emerging social media formats. All this marketing, along with the pressures of society, shape how we see ourselves. If you add the pressures of worldwide economic upheaval, high unemployment, changing moral values, and political unrest, it is no wonder people feel they are living lives of quiet, and sometimes not so quiet, desperation.

Chapter 6

Who am I, Really?

You probably know better than anyone else just how complex you are. If you give it any thought at all, you will also come to the conclusion that you are unique, a "one-of-a-kind." If you doubt that, let me employ a little of the Socratic method on you. Does anyone else have your DNA? Does anyone else have your fingerprints? Does anyone else have your retinal scan? The answer is "No" to all three of those questions. You are unique.

Your uniqueness extends to other areas that combine to make the real you. Some of these areas include:

- » Your personality
- » Your environment
- » Your experiences
- » Your education
- » Your career
- » Your family
- » Your ethnicity

- » Your race
- » Your socioeconomic status
- » Your culture
- » Where you grew up
- » When you were born

All of these, and a whole host of other factors, combine to make you the very unique person you are. So, on the surface, it may seem an easy question to answer, but down deep, it is actually very complex. Who are you, really?

Does anyone really know you as well as you know yourself? Probably not. However, other people can give you valuable insight by telling you things they see in you that you may not see. At one point in my business career, I left a position as a Vice President because I knew it was time to move on. The headhunter I enlisted to help me find another position specialized in placing former military officers. He asked me to send him copies of my last two Marine Corps evaluations. I hadn't thought of those evaluations in quite some time, so it took a while to find them. Before sending them to the headhunter, I re-read the evaluation comments of my former Commanding Officers. Man, was that revealing! At the time I originally received those reviews, I thought my COs were just being flattering, so I could get promoted. Now, looking back, I realize both Commanding Officers had been shrewd in their observations.

By the time the headhunter asked me to dig up those old evaluations, years of soul searching and research had gone into finding out who I really am. When I re-read comments from the commanding officers, I read from a position of really understanding my personality, my strengths, and how I think. If I had paid attention to what those two leaders said about me, and more importantly, taken the time to ask them some good questions, I would have saved myself at least ten years of wandering through several careers while trying to figure out what to do with my life.

Being married for twenty-six years to an absolutely great lady has also helped me tremendously in figuring out who I am. I am sure that during those twenty-six years, I have had periods where I was as great a mystery to Mary as she has been to me. The advantage of being with someone you love for that period of time is that he or she eventually figures you out. Input from a spouse, if you are brave and humble enough to take it, can be a valuable asset in answering the questions posed in this book. I remember asking Mary the question about who she thought I was, and she jokingly answered something such as, "I don't know, but would you please hurry up and figure it out, so I can figure out who I am!" It was kind of funny at the time, but it revealed a very important truth to me. Until I knew who I was, I was holding back others from knowing themselves, as well: one of those people was my wife. The quest to discover your real self is not selfish. As a matter of fact, it is actually quite selfish not to figure it out. Someone else is probably counting on you.

Chapter 7

Personality

Have you ever carefully watched small children? Can you pick out how different their personalities are? Most parents who have more than one child will tell you their children are very different from each other, and that their differences were noticed soon after birth.

Merriam-Webster's Collegiate Dictionary contains this interesting definition of "personality":

- » "the complex of characteristics that distinguishes an individual or a nation or a group;
- » the totality of an individual's behavioral and emotional tendencies;
- » the organization of the individual's distinguishing character traits, attitudes or habits."

So, this definition tells me that how you act, react, organize, and form habits is based on your personality. How you think is largely influenced by your personality.

Questions:

1. How did you get your personality?
2. Is yours better than someone else's?
3. Can you change your personality?
4. Can it be influenced?

Answers:

1. You were born with your personality. In addition to the gift of life, the Father gave you the gift of your personality. "Before I formed you in the womb, I knew you.[11]"
2. NO! Each person's personality is perfect for him or her. No one personality type is better than another.
3. NO! If you are hiding or masking your true personality, you can unmask it, but you cannot change how you were created. If it was a gift from the Father, why would you want to change it?
4. Yes! So be very careful who you let influence your personality.

So, if your personality affects the way you act, how you react to circumstances, how you organize your thoughts, how you form habits, and how you think about things, wouldn't it be a good idea to get as good of an understanding of your personality as you can? You will not be able to understand anyone else until you understand yourself. Once you know your own personality, you will be better able to understand how you are different from other people. This will become very important as we explore the questions in the following chapters.

Several institutions and authors have developed good methods for testing and categorizing personalities. The one I am most familiar with is DISC profiles. *Getting to Know You*[12], by Chris Carey, is an excellent book for learning about basic personality types. *Who Do You Think You*

---

11 The Holy Bible, Jeremiah 1:5

12 *Getting to Know You*, Chris Carrey

Are Anyway[13], a book by Robert Rohm, has an excellent section about the different blends of personalities and the characteristics of the different blends. There is also an online evaluation you can take which will give you a twenty page printout about your personality. It is based on your answers to 16 questions, and it is scary accurate!

DISC is an acronym that is a combination of the four major personality types.

D: "D" style people are

- » Dominant
- » Directing
- » Demanding
- » Doers

The D personalities are driven people. They are forceful in demeanor, and likely measure their success in life by wins and losses. They want to be in charge, they exert control, and they want to win. They get things started and keep them moving. They write books about goals, measure achievement by goals, and think everyone else should also. They are the least likely personality style to think one's personality makes any difference because everyone should be like them. They are the most likely personality style to be natural leaders. D personalities tend to see themselves as

- » Pioneering
- » Adventurous
- » Upbeat
- » Competitive
- » Fearless leaders

People who are not D personalities tend to see D personalities as

- » Domineering
- » Abrasive

---

13 *Who Do You Think You Are Anyway*, Robert Rohm

- » Rough
- » Firm
- » Risk takers

I: "I" type of personalities are

- » Influencing
- » Inspiring
- » Impulsive

I type personalities love to be around people, and they think everyone should like them. They like to be the center of attention and are usually very charming and fun to be around. I personalities are infamous for acting or talking first, and thinking later. If they have to bend (or completely ignore) the facts in order to inspire someone they have no qualms about it. If they make a mistake it would not be uncommon to hear them say something like, "it's okay, they'll still like me."

I once had a boss named Charlie (actually he was the president of the company) that was a very high I personality. Charlie loved going on sales calls and working at trade show booths, and I learned a lot from him. Charlie was one of the most liked people in his industry and everyone knew him. However, on some sales calls I wanted to find a hole and climb in because of some of the stuff he would say. If he was asked a question about a product that he didn't know, he would just make up things. He said it so convincingly, and with such great enthusiasm, that people just believed him. I remember calling him on it once, and he looked at me as if to say, "what's the big deal?"

I personalities see themselves as

- » Upbeat
- » Fun
- » Enthusiastic
- » Optimistic
- » Persuasive
- » Spontaneous

Other people sometimes see I personalities as

- » Overly Confident
- » Unrealistic
- » Talkative
- » Poor listeners
- » Self-promoting
- » Exaggerating
- » Unpredictable

S: The "S" style of personality is the most common of the four major styles. Approximately seventy-five percent of the population exhibits the S style as part of their dominant personality blend. They are people oriented and reserved in demeanor.

Words that describe an S personality are

- » Supportive
- » Steady
- » Sensitive
- » Stubborn

They like to belong to a team, they resist change, and don't want to rock the boat. They are great employees and crave peace and security. They want to be appreciated and to have a voice. S personalities like to build relationships, and they tend to think with their emotions. If pushed into a corner, the S personality can be very stubborn and be willing to fight, but they prefer peaceful solutions.

S personality types see themselves as

- » Considerate
- » Good listeners
- » Calm
- » Easy going

» Kind

» Team players

However, other personalities can see them as

» Hesitant

» Detached

» Unconcerned

» Inflexible

» Indecisive

Since they represent a large part of the population it would be important for the non-S personalities to bear in mind that these people may be slow starters that like to wait for instructions. However they are very loyal to their team, and they like to finish what they start.

Because S personalities can be very good listeners, and sensitive to the needs of others, I asked some high S types to read the manuscript for this book to get their perspective before I began the editing process. Boy was I glad I did. The S factor ranks very low on my own personality, so their input helped me to temper the way I wrote some things to be able to relate to a broader segment of the population.

Getting advice from S personalities also clued me in to how many people can be influenced by strong, charismatic personalities. A dominant personality with vision can target their message to S personalities who think emotionally. This could work for good, or it could work for bad, but it explains why so many marketing and political messages seem to appeal to our emotional side.

C: Words that describe the "C" style of personality are

» Cautious

» Calculating

» Contemplative

» Criticizing

» Conscientious

The C personality is likely to be the deepest thinker of the four types. They can also be accused of analysis paralysis because they want all the facts before making a decision. They have an overwhelming desire to be correct and hate to be told they are wrong. They make great planners and are very good at finding solutions to problems. They are the most likely personality style to take things personally or to hold a grudge. It is very stressful for them to be in disorganized surroundings or to work with people that are careless or untidy. They also desire to follow procedures, and want proof and evidence to make decisions.

C personalities see themselves as

» Conservative
» Logical
» Alert
» Conscientious
» Precise
» Thorough

Other personality types see Cs as

» Pessimistic
» Picky
» Fussy
» Hard to please
» Defensive
» Strict

Having a C type of personality on your team can be very valuable. They are the ones that are likely to provide critical analysis and comprehensive problem solving for your project. Because they want quality work and are deadline conscious, they are the ones that keep things on track and make it right. They also tend to be the team members that keep things "real" because they deal in facts.

When I think of the value that C personalities bring to business, I think of McDonalds. Their business procedures are so good that they can get teen-age employees to do things efficiently that their parents could only dream of. Since procedures that work are the keys to the success to any large and profitable business, we can thank the C personalities of the world because they are probably the ones who went through the pain staking work of developing those procedures.

> **CAUTION:**
> **your personality is not an excuse for bad character and not an excuse to**
> - » Be a jerk: "Well this is how I am, so just accept it."
> - » Be lazy: "I'm just not the ambitious type."
> - » Be a social misfit: "You know me, I'm just carefree."
> - » Regardless of your personality, you can be successful and of good character. The way in which you succeed and express your character will be influenced by your personality.

Before I go any further, it is important to know two things. First, no one personality is better than another. Your personality is perfect for you. Second, no one is 100 percent of any of the four basic types. We are blends of these types of personalities. Understanding your blend will give you some very good insight into who you really are. Understanding other people's blends will give you insight into who they really are, and allow you to understand people on a better level. Ultimately, your success in life and the fulfillment of your quest will depend on not just yourself, but on other people, as well. It would be a huge mistake to assume everyone thinks and acts like you do. Understanding the different personality styles can make all the difference for you.

You can determine your basic style by answering a couple of questions, however, I recommend you take an online profile test at www.personalityinsights.com or www.thediscpersonalitytest.com to get a more complete understanding of your particular blend. So here are the basic questions.

You may be more one way than another, depending on the

circumstances, and you may be fifty-one percent one way and forty-nine percent the other, but generally, if no one else is around to influence you, would you say that you are more outgoing, or more reserved? If you say you are more outgoing than reserved, then your basic personality style is at the top half of the chart below. If you are more reserved than outgoing, then your basic personality is on the lower half of the chart.

Again, you may be more one way than another, depending on the circumstances, and you may be fifty-one percent one way and forty-nine percent the other, but generally, if no one else is around to influence you, would you say that you are more task-oriented or more people-oriented? If you are more task-oriented than people-oriented, then your basic personality is on the left side of the chart. If you are more people-oriented than task-oriented, your basic style is on the right side of the chart.

So, for example, if you are an outgoing, task-oriented person, your dominant personality style is that of a D personality. If you are a more reserved, people-oriented person, then you have a dominant personality style of an S personality.

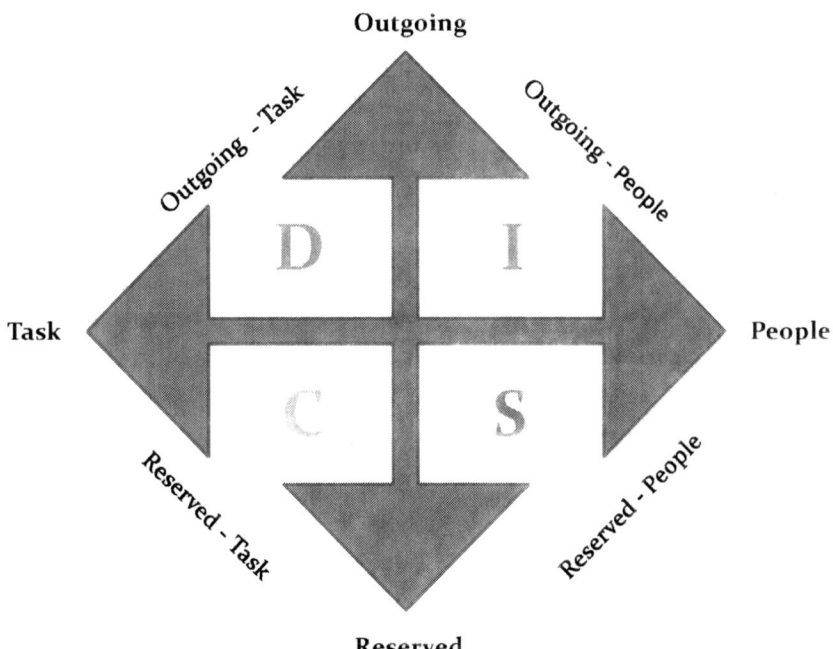

Finding out what your dominant personality style is, and understanding your particular blend of personality, will help you realize how unique you really are. It may also explain a few mysteries in your life as well.

I have a friend—I'll call him Bob—who has a high C type personality. Bob is not naturally an outgoing person. He has an aviation background, which his personality lends itself to very well. He is cautious, calculating, and precise and he hates making mistakes. He is somewhat of a thinker, and if you tell him he is wrong about something, he will take it very personally; then he will think over the "something" in every possible direction. Bob decided to leave aviation and begin a business that was very people-oriented. His new business required that he make live presentations to groups of people and become an expert salesman. By sheer force of will, he is making it work. Bob believes that if he can just get the sales process down to a science, he will become tremendously successful. Fortunately for Bob, he is married to "Betty." Betty has a high I personality. She loves everyone, and everyone loves her. Betty is a gifted sales person because of her love for people. Bob and Betty are almost exact opposites on the personality chart, and once they learned to work together, their overlapping personalities covered almost all the chart. By that, I mean that their personality blends—while being strong in the C and I quadrants—also have enough of the other major personality types in their blends to be relatable to almost everyone. The best marriages seem to work that way—opposites attracting each other. The trick is learning not to kill each other until you learn how to work together.

Most successful sales-related businesses are populated by D and I personality blends. That is because they are more outgoing, and either goal- oriented or people-oriented. Bob actually chose a business for which he was not well suited. The part of his business he likes, and the part he tends to spend the majority of his time in, involves improving processes. That is a very C-like trait. Whether he becomes as successful as he would like to be is still a question. If Bob had found a business that could use more of his C-like traits, he would probably find his work easier, and a lot more enjoyable.

My wife is a very high D personality. When Mary was in the Navy, she was put in charge of a group of Chief Petty Officers who were experts in ship repair and engineering. The group's task was to determine what repairs had to be made on the aircraft carriers home-ported in San Diego. Mary used to brag about never having taken a science or math class in college, and here she was in charge of engineering decisions for many millions of dollars that determined aircraft carrier readiness. Her D personality traits kicked into high gear, and she became so good at getting her personnel to perform that she was recognized as the San Diego Naval Woman of the Year. She loved her job and her people thought she was an awesome leader.

On the other hand, a D personality that is not using their D traits can be like a ticking time bomb. A friend of mine—I'll call him David—is a high D personality who is literally sick because he is not being himself. David was a very successful leader in the Marines, but since leaving the military he has been in detail oriented jobs, trying to please bosses that only think they are leaders. Consequently, David has been incredibly frustrated in most of the positions he has had for the last ten years. While his bosses had trouble making even simple decisions, David can lead and decide quickly, but has been relegated to crunching numbers. David took the personality test, and finally understands why he is frustrated and stressed in his career life. He is beginning to understand how he is wired, and that his personality is a gift from God designed for him to succeed. David is taking a fresh look at what he wants to do with his life. The true leader in him is beginning to emerge. Now he needs to find a position where he can be in charge, and drive results.

Sometimes, we subconsciously mask our personalities by trying to be people we are not. That is what I did. My parents both loved people and loved being around them—my dad, in particular. He enjoyed going to parties, having a few drinks, and being the life of the party. He loved telling jokes and making people laugh. At family reunions, everyone sought him out for advice, not so much for his sage wisdom but because they always felt loved by him. Dad could be loud, forceful, and loving all at the same time. He was my hero.

My personality is nothing like his. I much prefer a quiet setting with my best friend, Mary. At a party, I am always looking for an exit. I had to learn how to be sociable and had to cultivate people skills in order to function in society, but it did not come naturally to me. Since I admired my father so much, I found myself trying to mold my personality into one like his. In college, I went to all the parties, only to be bored. I tried to be one of the boys in the squadron by going out to bars and laughing it up with the guys, only to have my jokes go flat and wonder why I felt out of place. I tried to be a forceful, charismatic leader, but only came off sounding arrogant. All of those missteps came from trying to be something I was not. I don't want to sound like I was a social misfit, because that was not the case, but as soon as I owned up to my real self, and stopped trying to be something I was not, I relaxed around people. Then people relaxed around me.

Since I have personal experience in personality masking, I can recognize that trait in others. It is painful to watch someone cover up who he really is and watch him be unaware of what he is doing. Being yourself is much more fun and liberating. It is interesting to note that the one who is masking his true self cannot blame anyone but himself. My father certainly was not trying to mold me into his image. I did that on my own volition. I have counseled people who tell me their parents forced them to be different from who they really were, but the truth is usually different from their perceptions. I have also counseled parents who tried to force their personalities on their children. Once they recognized their own personalities and the personalities of their children, their parenting changed almost overnight and became fun again. Even though many marriage challenges are about money, most are about one person not recognizing differences between their own personality and that of their spouse.

As you can probably tell, I am a big proponent of you knowing your personality style. It is an important part of fulfilling your quest, and it will probably be a fun learning experience to identify your personality type. I strongly recommend you take one of the online personality tests and share your results with the person you trust most in life. You will be pleasantly surprised at the discussion your openness will generate.

Chapter 8

Who's Your Daddy?

Gregory Dickow is the pastor of Life Changers International Church located in the suburbs of Chicago. I give him credit for coining the term "Father Fracture" and teaching how destructive a father fracture can be. The sad fact is that almost everyone has a father fracture to some degree, so before dismissing the idea, please allow me to explain the term.

A Father Fracture is when:

1. You had a bad relationship (or no relationship) with your father. This will probably lead to you having a difficult time having a good relationship (or any relationship, for that matter) with your Father (God).
2. If you didn't receive the unconditional love that your father was supposed to give you, you will have no example by which to fully recognize the unconditional love your Father has for you.
3. Your identity is derived from your relationship with your father. He is supposed to point you to your Father who created you just as He desired.

Hollywood movies often mirror what is happening in society. Some of my favorite movies are Gladiator, The Kingdom of Heaven, the Star Wars movies, and the Lord of the Rings trilogy. All of these have huge Father Fractures as part of their themes. Mary likes the romantic "chick flicks," and almost all of them have Father Fractures running through their plots. It seems that Hollywood may be telling us something.

According to Pastor Dickow, most of us get our identities from our fathers. That statement can be emotionally packed, but I think it is true. Our mothers are usually the ones who nurture us. Our desire to please our mothers stems from the need for security. Mothers are the ones we can run to for sympathy when something is wrong, or to make a boo-boo feel better. If you had a good mother, she probably hugged you and made you feel loved. She was probably your biggest supporter and was always on your side. She made sure you had food, shelter, and basic necessities, and she tried to make you feel secure. I seldom hear people telling me they feel negatively about their mothers. It would be a very rare exception to hear someone say they felt abandoned by his or her mother. It does happen, but for the most part, if parents split up, the children usually end up with the mother.

According to U.S. Census Bureau 2009 statistics

- » 26% of children under 21 are in a single parent home
- » Of that, 84% of the custodial parents are mothers
- » 50% of all children will live in a single parent home at sometime before they reach age 18

Many people I speak with today grew up in single-parent families. They consider single-parent families "normal." If you were fortunate to have a father in your home when you grew up, let me ask you the following questions. Was your father really there? Did he help you, guide you, and provide leadership in your family? Or did your mom do those things? Even families with two parents often have a dad who is actually absent for the children. Does any of this relate to you?

Both Bob and David from the examples in chapter seven have a father fracture. Bob's dad verbally abused him as a child and then left his mother and him when Bob was young. I am not sure what happened in David's case, but David assumed he and his father had a great relationship. When I asked him how often his father told him he loved him, or that he was proud of him, David said, "Never"—not even when David received his pilot wings. David said he didn't have "that kind of a relationship" with his father. That statement baffled me. What kind of relationship did he think he was supposed to have? The more I checked into this question, the more I realized **most men and women don't know what a proper relationship with their father is supposed to look like.** That is mostly because they have never seen one.

I asked my wife about this and was surprised by her answer. Her dad died when she was a teenager. Prior to his passing away from a heart attack, he and Mary's mother were separated. There was major tension in their home and a lot of stress and alcohol abuse. So, when I asked Mary what she thought a good relationship with a father should look like, she told me she saw it in my father. In fact, she told me how awesome it was for her to see my mother sitting in my father's lap the first time she came over to our home. Having grown up in a home with a strong and loving father, I took it for granted. My late dad was by no means perfect, but he is still the best example I know for what a father is supposed to be.

The interesting thing about my dad is that he had a huge father fracture of his own. Something went ugly wrong in his home. As a teenager, he left home after his tenth grade year and joined the Marine Corps. That year was 1940, and since the U.S. had not yet entered World War II, he didn't join the Marines out of patriotic fervor. He just wanted to get out of his home situation. Apparently, his father had not gotten along too well with his mother, and his father had a bad habit of spending his paycheck on drinking and "playing the ponies." As the middle of six kids in a rough neighborhood in Philadelphia, my father needed to escape. By the time I came along, Dad had fought in World War II and Korea. He was the picture of the perfect marine first sergeant; he had a booming command voice and all the medals to go with it. If he looked into your eyes, you would swear he could look right into your soul. It was impossible to lie to him.

My earliest memory of my father is of the day I thought he was going to kill me. I was four years old, and we lived on Quantico Marine Base in Virginia. Dad was a company first sergeant at the time. The military home we lived in was an old town house that had a concrete stoop in front of its front door. Behind our house stood an entire row of similar kinds of townhouses, but those had five or six steps that led up to glass storm doors. That row of houses was abandoned, and the entire street was empty—except for me.

I have no idea why, but at four years of age, I had a fascination with breaking glass. I loved to break Coke bottles or light bulbs whenever I got a chance. It was nothing malicious, mind you. I just thought breaking glass was great fun. Well, one day while Dad was at work and Mom wasn't looking, I walked to the abandoned street behind our home. Right in front of me appeared a brick that was perfect for a four-year-old to throw. With great excitement, I walked up the five steps leading to a glass storm door in front of one of those abandoned townhouses, and just as the brick was leaving my hand, a military policeman (also known as an MP) rounded the street corner in his car. Still oblivious to the MP's presence, but with great joy, I watched the glass door shatter into what seemed like a million pieces. The MP probably watched the whole thing in disbelief. The only thing he asked me before he made me get into the police car, was where I lived. When he knocked at the front door of our home, he had my tiny arm in his big hand, and he had no concern for the tears streaming down my face. I can't imagine what my mother thought.

Mom is German. She had only lived in the U.S. for five years, at that time, and her English wasn't all that good. On top of that, Dad's first assignment after they got married had been recruiting duty in Scranton, Pennsylvania, so this was her first experience with Marine Corps life on a military base. Seeing her son being held by a Military Policeman was too much for her. So, Mom called Dad at work and told him to come home because an MP was at the door. She didn't know what to do with me, so she sent me to my room on the second floor. I sat on the edge of my bed with my little legs hanging over, just waiting for my dad to come home. I was sure I would never see my fifth birthday.

Dad walked slowly up the stairs. By that time, I was too scared to cry. He appeared in the doorway, and I looked up at the six-foot, one-inch Marine First Sergeant who was my father. Dad, at that time, had a forty-six-inch chest and a thirty-inch waist. He was dressed in his khaki uniform; his shirt full of decorations from wars he had fought in. He looked at me with his best Drill Instructor gaze and asked, "Did you do this?" As I told you, it was impossible to lie to him, so I said "Yes." Then he asked, "Are you sorry?" Of course, I said yes, again. "Are you ever going to do that again?" was his next question, and, of course, I said no. Then the unexpected happened. Dad burst out laughing and had to leave the room because he couldn't stop. I don't remember what happened after that, probably because the pressure was off. That was the day I learned that there really was a God, and that He was merciful, because I sure deserved whatever I might have gotten.

This same tough, rugged, highly respected man tucked my sister and me into bed every night. Before we were tucked in, my mom, my sister, my dad, and I would all kneel down by our beds to say prayers. Every night Dad would ask me if I was warm enough, and then he'd kiss me before he left the room. I never once had to guess if I was loved by my parents.

As I grew, Dad was always there for me. I remember, as a teenager, agreeing to take another guy's Sunday morning paper route for him while he went on vacation. At four a.m. on a Sunday morning, I waited on a corner a block away from our house for newspapers to be dropped off. It was dark, I had no flashlight, and rain began to fall. I had no idea what I was doing. So, I walked home with the papers and sat in the kitchen, crying as I started to wrap the newspapers in plastic. I didn't want to wake up Dad, because I wanted him to be proud of me, not see me looking like a basket case. Dad must have heard me, because he dressed and came downstairs. He never complained about the time or told me how stupid I was; he just helped me deliver the papers. When we were done, he put his arm around me and then went back to bed. Needless to say, I didn't last as a paperboy.

Bob and David did not have those kinds of experiences with their fathers; neither did my wife. Only after hearing Pastor Dickow speak about the Father Fracture did I realize how truly blessed I was to have grown up with a real father. No matter what I did, or did not do, my father always told me how proud he was of me and that he loved me. He gave me my identity as an approved son of a great man.

In order to give you a better appreciation of my opinion of what a father should be, I wrote the following:

Father

As a Child

You loved me before I could love you in return

You hugged me and kissed me and told me you loved me

You prayed with me

You protected me

You gave me security

You provided for me

You gave me gifts

You taught me

You comforted me

You provided stability

You corrected me

You reproved me

You taught me the only thing I needed to fear was you

You were like God:

All powerful, all knowing, always present

Even when I walked down the dark alley, I did not fear, because you were with me

You gave me a firm foundation

As an adolescent

You loved me

You prayed for me

You coached me

You showed me it was OK to make mistakes

You showed me how to say "I am sorry"

You guided me

You taught me respect

You told me you were proud of me

You approved of me without my having to earn it

You were my advocate

You tested me

You built my self-esteem

You gave me confidence

You made things right when I messed up

You were available to me without reproof

You saved me from destruction

You protected me from my peers

You allowed me to grow

As a Young man

You loved me

You prayed for me

You counseled me

You comforted me

You showed me how to have a good marriage

You allowed me to question you

You provided a safe haven in times of stress

You guided me on the right path

You gave me wings to find my own way

You blessed me

As an adult

You loved me

You prayed with me

You were my friend

You put your arm around me
You became a part of me
You became my example

When you died
You told me that one can never love too much
You saw angels
You showed me you were indeed like God
Because of you, I know Him
He is our Father
Thanks, Dad!

I fully realize that some of you who are reading this had a father as good as mine, or better. But most of you did not. If you will recall, I said earlier that your information is as only as good as the questions you ask, and that before you can get where you are going, you have to know where you are starting from. Randy Thornton, pastor of Grace Church in Southern Pines, North Carolina put it succinctly when he said that a child has two overarching questions they need answered: "Who loves me?", and "Who is in charge?" Realizing that you have a Father Fracture is ninety percent of the battle. Until you deal with it, you will not have a firm foundation from which to move forward.

The following are some telltale signs that you have a Father Fracture. (Please note that any one of them could be devastating to you and could leave scars that interfere with your knowing your real self. Please also note that I am not making any judgmental statements about your situation.)

1. You never knew your father
2. Your father abandoned your family
3. Your father died when you were young
4. Your father was in the home but not there for you
5. Your parents divorced
6. Your father never, or rarely, told you he loved you

7. You felt that you had to earn his approval
8. You felt that you had to earn his love
9. Your father never corrected you
10. Your mother did not respect your father
11. You had feelings of insecurity as a child
12. You were physically or emotionally abused
13. You are promiscuous now

When you have had the approval of your father, without having had to earn it, you have a source of confidence that lasts a lifetime. When you KNOW you are loved by your father, no matter what you do or don't do, the natural result is to want to please him. You won't need anyone else's approval to make you feel complete. Having your dad tell you he is proud of you, and that his pride is not coming from your performance, instills a sense of pride in you that no one can remove. For whatever reason, these things are more important, and have a greater effect on you when they come from your father than from your mother. Somehow, mothers are expected to have these feelings and say these things to their children, and it is vitally important to us to have them from our mothers. But if a person doesn't get them from their father, a very important piece of their identity is missing.

Ultimately, a good father has one crucial task. By being a good father—one who loves, approves, protects, provides for, teaches, and guides his children—a father teaches his children about the nature of God. Jesus always referred to God as "Father." No matter how good or bad our fathers were, our Father (with a capitol "F") is really the one doing the loving, approving, protecting, providing, teaching and guiding. Eventually, your father (if you have one) will die and leave you, but your Father will never leave you or forsake you. So, if you have a Father Fracture, the one you can always turn to is your Father, not your father. Even Jesus learned this as a young man. We don't know when, but at some point, Joseph (Jesus' earthly "stepdad', and apparently a very good man) died. Jesus always referred to God as his Father. In fact, he sometimes called him "Abba," which is translated "daddy." When Jesus taught us to pray, the first two words he used were "Our Father." This is no accident.

Religion will not teach you this. Religion is all about control, rules, conduct, guilt, and fear. Jesus was all about the relationship he had with His Father; our Father. My dad never made me feel guilty. Neither does my Abba. That is not to say that I never did things wrong and needed to ask my dad's forgiveness, but, heck, he loved me, so I knew he would forgive me, even before I asked him. Asking for his forgiveness made us both feel better so that the air was clear between us. It is exactly the same way with your Father. How awesome is that?

If you have never done this, I would encourage you to pull out a Bible and find out for yourself when Jesus started doing miracles. What you will find (in Matthew chapter 3, Mark chapter 1 and Luke chapter 3) is that Jesus heard his Father tell him that he (God the Father) was well pleased with him BEFORE Jesus ever did anything great—even before Jesus was tempted in the desert. So, it wasn't Jesus' actions that gained the Father's approval. It was just the fact that Jesus was the Father's son. You have the same privilege. As Pastor Dickow says, "You have not heard the voice of God until you have heard the voice of Love." Your Father is waiting for you. Heal the Father Fracture and know what it is like to be loved and approved by your Father. He has so much more he wants to give you and show you.

Chapter 9

How You Give and Receive Love

Before leaving the first question about *who you really are*, I would be remiss if I didn't cover this very vital piece of the puzzle. In his book *The Five Love Languages*[14], Gary Chapman tells us that we don't all give or receive love the same way. When I first read his book, I was amazed. I didn't think there was anything new that I could discover about my wife or our marriage. Obviously that wasn't true, because I learned about her personality and strengths (which we will cover in another part of the book) after about twenty years of being married to her. So, discovering that we gave and received love differently shouldn't have been a surprise. But it was.

Just like your personality and all the other factors that combine to make you so unique, your way of loving is unique. Gary Chapman boils love languages down to five different types, but just as with the four major types of personalities, each person is a blend. He says that we primarily love in one of these five ways:

» by giving and receiving gifts

---

14 *The Five Love Languages*, Gary Chapman

- » by acts of service
- » by spending quality time
- » by physical touch or
- » by words of affirmation

If someone gives you a gift, no matter how small or large the gift, and that makes you feel special and loved, then your love language may be gifts. If someone doing things for you makes you feel especially appreciated, then acts of service may be your love language. When just being in the same room doing nothing in particular, or being together on a road trip makes you feel special, then quality time is your love language. If holding hands, a back rub, or a head massage tells you that, no matter what else is going on, he still loves you, then physical touch may be your love language. If your heart warms when she tells you how much she appreciates you, and that you are great in her eyes, then your love language may be words of affirmation.

One language is not better than another, and you may actually have a couple languages that stand out for you, but one will be your dominant language. It is important to remember that just because you receive love in a certain way, does not necessarily mean that the one you love receives love in the same way. In fact, that would be rare. So, not only do you need to be aware of your own language, but you need to be able to speak the language of the one you love. I am laughing inside as I think of the mistakes I have made with Mary in this area. When we were newly married, we lived in Encinitas, California. Florists from all over the country purchased the beautiful flowers that grew on Encinitas hills. On any back road around Encinitas you could find flower stands selling bouquets of locally grown flowers at really good prices. Being the loving husband, and trying to show my new wife how much I thought of her, I would frequently stop at a flower stand and buy an arrangement, then put it in a vase on our dining room table for her. Now, I should tell you I am not a flower guy, and giving or receiving gifts is not my love language. I was doing this for Mary because I had seen in movies and on TV that girls really like this kind of stuff.

Several weeks went by and not a peep from Mary. So, I finally mustered the courage to bring it up to my new bride. I asked her if she liked the flowers. Her response was, "Oh my goodness, I didn't even see them. Those are nice. Thank you." That was it! So I did a very intelligent thing. I didn't get offended, but asked her if gifts or flowers really did anything for her. She liked flowers, but only if she grew them in her garden. As far as gifts went, they were certainly appreciated, but she did not need them to tell her I loved her. I am a lucky man!

I discovered her love language by accident. We had an awesome Italian restaurant close to where we lived, and Friday night pizza was a ritual for me. We would often find ourselves at Papachino's restaurant in Del Mar, waiting for a table on Friday nights. Usually, Mary would be exhausted from a week's work, and she would put her legs up on my lap as we waited. I started giving her a foot massage, and I think she went to heaven. She kept saying, "Oh, that feels so good," over and over. One of the waitresses heard her and looked right at me and asked, "Do you have a brother?" I guess the waitress' love language was physical touch, as was Mary's. Notice, I didn't say groping or having sex when I said physical touch. To this day, no matter how tense things might be between us, if I scratch her back or her head before we go to sleep, Mary knows I still love her and that everything is good between us.

I have a good friend who likes massages, so he has a habit of giving people shoulder massages as a form of greeting. Many people really like it, but I am not one of them. I finally had to tell him I loved him like a brother, but if he ever tried to give me another shoulder massage, I was going to break his hands. Physical touch is NOT my love language. For me to give love in this way to my wife is an effort. I know how much it means to her, so I am happy to give her love in the form she needs. Even though I sort of knew her love language after years of being together, it wasn't really confirmed until we read *The Five Love Languages*. Mary wasn't sure of my language until she read the book and we had a chance to discuss it together. I'm one of those people who likes order, and I am visually oriented. Seeing things out of place in our home, or seeing our home become dirty really bothers me. Mary often doesn't even notice the things that bug me. Remember, she didn't see the flowers, either. So, in order to keep a sense of order in our home, I started picking up and doing a lot of the cleaning in our house. She told me she thought I was doing this as an act of service for her, which is not her love language at all. I finally had to set her straight. I wasn't doing those things for her; I was doing them for me. If she did them, I would appreciate it, but I would really just like the sense of order, not the idea that she was doing something for me.

It is sad, but we have all heard the stories of couples who have been married for a long time and then divorce. Sometimes, they hang on until their children leave the nest, or sometimes they are in their sixties and just can't stay together longer. There is a story in *The Five Love Languages* about a couple like this. The man reached the end of his rope, but agreed to get some marriage counseling before they called it quits. In counseling, he said that he just couldn't please her. He did this for her, and he did that for her, and she never appreciated him for it. Obviously, his love language was acts of service. His wife, on the other hand, told him that all she ever wanted was to spend time with him. Sitting on the couch together, or watching TV or a movie would have meant the world to her, but he was always too busy fixing cars or doing this or that. Here were two people who had been together for over forty years, and neither of them knew how they needed to receive love.

How do you give and receive love? Don't you think it would be a good idea to know this about yourself? Fortunately, there are several tools that can aid you in figuring it out. If you search the Internet for *Five Love Languages Quiz*, you will find several free quizzes that take just a few minutes to complete. Your reply will be immediate, and you won't have to guess. If you are married, or are thinking of being married, I would recommend you have the other person take the quiz also. It should be revealing, and it could save you a lot of heartache.

There is another aspect of giving love that is important. As a D and C personality blend, my personality profile has described me as being cold, critical and aloof—not exactly words that I would regard as being praiseworthy, nor are they very loving in nature. It took me a while to reconcile that those descriptive words were actually pretty accurate. I wanted, and actually prayed for, help in becoming more loving and compassionate towards people. The problem was I was not wired that way, and being loving and compassionate was real effort and unnatural for me. Then I discovered something that resolved my dilemma. Until I got okay with who I really was, there was no way I would discover my gift (the subject of part III of *The Holy Hand Grenade*). Once I discovered my gift and began to develop it and give it away, I then learned how I was meant to be compassionate and loving. In the process of using my gift, my compassion, patience, and love flow without effort. The more I use my gift, the more these virtues became evident. So, if you are having a difficult time being the loving person you want to be, my advice would be to first get good with who you really are—then discover your gift.

Chapter 10

How You Think

The first question, "Who am I, really?" has a lot to do with the way you think. You will find this trend written about from several perspectives throughout this book. For those of us who like hard evidence, there has been some amazing new research into how the brain functions to create thoughts and store memory. Dr. Caroline Leaf has a PhD in Communication Pathology and has dedicated her life to helping people understand how their brains work. She has written a bestselling book, *Who Switched Off My Brain?*[15], and another book called *The Gift in You*[16].

I had a difficult time determining where to place this information in *The Holy Hand Grenade* because it really pertains to all three questions. I agree with Dr. Leaf that how you think is an integral and unique part of who you are. That is why this information is placed here. Ninety percent of your life happens between your ears, so how you think is the greatest part of who you really are.

---

15 *Who Switched Off My Brain*, Dr. Caroline Leaf
16 *The Gift in You*, Dr. Caroline Leaf

Have you ever talked with a friend about an event you both went to, and it seems as if you had completely different experiences? It could be doing something as simple as driving a car. My wife and I recently took a road trip and encountered some pretty heavy traffic driving through Richmond, Virginia. We hit rush hour on a curvy part of the highway that had traffic backed up. The pilot in me came out, and I saw it as a chance to use some combat techniques to weave through the cars. Mary hates driving in traffic, so she was having no fun at all. Of course, my aggressive driving probably didn't help much, but to me it was a challenge and a nice break from boring highway driving. So, here were two people in the same car, during the same event, but how we thought about it gave us two different experiences.

Dr. Leaf describes how your senses pick up information and how your brain processes it. The really interesting thing about her scientifically proven research is that it shows this: we don't all think the same way. How you process information picked up by your senses is pretty unique to you. As with personality tests, she has developed a test that can help you understand the primary way your brain is wired. Understanding how your brain is wired will help you in several ways. It will help you understand the best way for you to learn. It will help you figure out what kinds of professions you might might be better suited to, and it will help you understand what blocks your brain from receiving information and storing it as memory.

Dr. Leaf discovered there are seven basic types of thought. She calls them the Seven Pillars of thought. Each type of thought takes place in a different area in the brain. She says everyone uses all seven types of thought, but they seem to take precedence in an order that depends on how we are wired. There are normally two types of thought that will be dominant for you, and the others fall in line behind them. Discovering your dominant thought types can be very useful in adding to a complete picture of who you really are.

The Seven Pillars of thought are;

1. Intrapersonal thinking
2. Interpersonal thinking

3. Linguistic thinking
4. Logical/Mathematical thinking
5. Kinesthetic thinking
6. Musical thinking
7. Visual/Spatial thinking

Seven Pillar of Thought

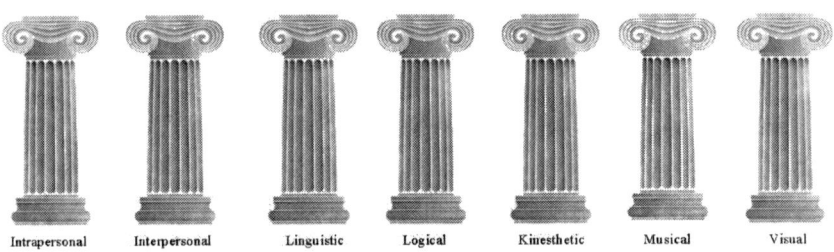

1. **Intrapersonal**

If your dominant way of thinking is intrapersonal, then you will receive information best by reflection and introspection.

Some of the characteristics of intrapersonal thinkers are:

» They have the ability to control their thoughts and emotions
» They prefer to work independently
» They are curious about the meaning of life
» They empower and encourage others

Some professions that usually have people with high intrapersonal thought are

» Judge
» Counselor
» Teacher
» Philosopher
» Visionary leader

2. **Interpersonal**

If your dominant way of thinking is interpersonal, then you will receive information best by communicating.

Some of the characteristics of interpersonal thinkers are:

- They have the ability to understand and work well with people
- They like social interaction and building relationships
- They are good at mediating disputes
- They love to talk

Some professions that usually have people with high interpersonal thought are:

- Politician
- Religious leader
- Salesperson
- Human Resources Manager

3. **Linguistic**

If your dominant way of thinking is linguistic, then words (spoken, written, expressed, or read) are how you primarily build memory.

Some of the characteristics of linguistic thinkers are:

- They care about semantics
- They like to argue and persuade
- They have a good memory for names, dates and places
- They ask a lot of questions

Some professions that usually have people with high linguistic thought are:

- Editor
- Speech Writer

- » Journalist
- » Speech/language therapist

4. **Logical/Mathematical**

If your dominant way of thinking is logical/mathematical, then reasoning is primarily how you build memory.

Some of the characteristics of logical/mathematical thinkers are:

- » They have the ability to manipulate and use numbers effectively
- » They like to reason things out
- » They like to identify and find meanings in things
- » They are intuitive and disciplined in their thinking

Some professions that usually have people with high logical/mathematical thought are:

- » Medical Doctor
- » Mathematician
- » Computer Programmer
- » Engineer

5. **Kinesthetic**

If your dominant way of thinking is kinesthetic, then movement and touch are how you primarily build memory.

Some of the characteristics of kinesthetic thinkers are:

- » They need to move when thinking
- » They have good coordination
- » They enjoy exercise
- » They have a good sense of timing

Some professions that usually have people with high kinesthetic thought are:

- » Athletes
- » Actors
- » Dancers
- » Mechanics

6. **Musical**

If your dominant way of thinking is musical, then you primarily build memory through rhythm and intuition.

Some of the characteristics of musical thinkers are:

- » They have the ability to read people through tone of voice and body language
- » They instinctively feel when things are right or wrong
- » They interpret the meaning behind things
- » They respond to music

Some professions that usually have people with high musical thought are:

- » Composer
- » Conductor
- » Public speaker
- » Musician

7. **Visual/Spatial**

If your dominant way of thinking is visual/spatial, then you primarily build memory through abstract language and imagery.

Some of the characteristics of visual/spatial thinkers are:

- » They navigate through spaces (traffic) well
- » They recognize faces, but may not remember names
- » They think in pictures and visualize details
- » They stare off into space when listening to someone

Some professions that usually have people with high visual/spatial thought are:

» Graphic designer
» Sculptor
» Photographer
» Pilot

These descriptions of the Seven Pillars of thought are very brief. I certainly recommend Dr. Leaf's books and DVDs to anyone who is interested in how the brain works and how you can make it work better. You can get more information at www.drleaf.com.

The different pillars of thought made me think of people in my life who exemplified some of these thought patterns. A friend of mine from my Marine Corps days was a member of the same staff meetings that I had to attend every week. This guy was a combination of linguistic and interpersonal thinking. It was as if someone would push a button on him somewhere during the staff meeting, and he would just start to talk. Ninety-five percent of what he said was just babble, but the other five percent was sheer brilliance. Most of us learned after a while that it was worth suffering through the ninety-five percent to get to the five percent. I can't help smiling at the thought of him talking, and of how many times we had to tell him to shut up. It really was pretty funny.

Dr. Leaf describes one of the CEOs she worked with that was a kinesthetic thinker. He had to be moving in order to operate. As you can imagine, this probably drove some of his co-workers nuts. Her solution was to have him sit on a big rubber ball instead of a chair, and it worked. I might recommend that solution to a friend of mine who cannot stand still. If he is standing in any one place for more than a couple of seconds, he has to start rocking, as if he is standing on the deck of a ship that is rolling with the waves. I get seasick just looking at him.

My dad was definitely a visual/spatial thinker. He could literally see something in his mind that he was going to build before he started. He was also a gifted artist. Before he began a portrait, he could actually see the finished painting. His final career as a graphic artist fit his thinking style well.

As I studied about how the brain works, I was amazed to learn a couple of things. First, there is a vast amount of new, scientifically proven evidence about how thoughts are formed in a human brain. Second, the way we think is so unique. Dr. Leaf's research even shows how identical twins think differently. The way your brain functions is a gift. Getting a better understanding of how to use that gift can make a big difference in answering the questions in the following chapters.

Chapter 11

Confidence

CONFIDENCE IS DEFINED AS A feeling of being conscious of one's powers. Confidence is a state of mind or a manner that is marked by an easy coolness and freedom from uncertainty. It means having faith in oneself and one's powers without any suggestion of conceit or arrogance. The interesting thing about people who exude confidence is that we are either drawn to them, or repelled by them. Being drawn or repelled by a confident person has as much to do with their purpose, as with their confidence (we will discuss this in chapter 29).

Napoleon Hill is a famous personal development and self-help author who wrote from about 1928 to 1970. His writings about the subject of success come from twenty-five years of studying, and living with, the greatest industrialists and businessmen of the industrial era. He is widely recognized as an authoritative writer, and his books are on the reading lists of most of the Fortune 500 CEOs. Hill says, "supreme self-confidence is based upon faith in God.[17]" He goes on to say, "faith begins where there is born within the heart a strong conviction that there is someone or something that is certain and can be trusted. This something must be

---

17 *How to Raise Your Own Salary*, Napoleon Hill

personal in every way. Faith can get you to where God intended you to be. Where you belong is as individual a place as you are an individual person. There is a special place, a special job for each of us…therefore, by believing in God, you begin to believe in yourself. Faith is essentially thought: thus, every call to have faith is a call to trust in the power of your own thought about the Creator…Then Believing in God, believing in ourselves, we begin to believe in our fellowman. Then harmony may begin.[18]" These are strange statements from a business writer who many believe was not a Christian. As I said in the introduction, you can't deny the truth—truth will set you free.

Hill's conclusion that confidence comes from faith lines up with the definition of confidence. In order to be confident, you have to have faith in something, or someone that is certain. I think most of us can relate to having placed our confidence in someone, only to be disappointed. Whenever you place your faith in a person, one thing is for certain: you will be disappointed sooner or later. Finding someone, something, that is worthy of your trust, your faith, and someone in whom you can have confidence will ultimately lead you to your Father. He made you to be the person you are, and he did it on purpose, and with purpose. Once you resolve that in your heart, you will have the kind of confidence that no man can shake.

So, confidence comes from knowing who you really are. When you know beyond a shadow of doubt who you are, how you think, and how you are wired, you can be confident in your actions. There is a proverb that says, "The righteous are bold as a lion.[19]" So, if you would like to have some boldness in life, read this story about the lion.

The Lion

The lion is known far and wide as the king of the jungle. He is bold and confident, and knows his rightful place in the animal kingdom. One day, he felt the need to reaffirm his position as he walked through his kingdom. The first animal he came upon was a mighty gorilla. The lion

---

18 *Succeed and Grow Rich Through Persuasion*, Napoleon Hill

19 *The Holy Bible*, Proverbs 28:1

asked, "Mr. Gorilla, who am I?" The gorilla replied, "Why, you are the Lion, king of the jungle."

The lion let out a loud roar that could be heard for miles because he approved of the gorilla's answer.

Next the lion approached a zebra. He asked the zebra the same question. "Mr. Zebra, who am I?" To which the zebra replied, "Why, you are the Lion, king of the jungle."

The lion let out another loud roar that could be heard for miles because he approved of the zebra's answer.

Walking a little further, the lion approached a huge elephant. He asked, "Mr. Elephant, do you know who I am?" The elephant didn't say a word. Instead he calmly reached out with his massive trunk and grabbed the lion by the tail. Then, with no warning, he twirled the lion through the air, smashed him on the ground and threw him twenty feet into a boulder. The lion, a little dazed and battered, walked back up to the elephant and told him, "Look, just because you didn't know the answer, doesn't mean you have to get all testy about it!"

The lion knew who he was, and he was not about to let the elephant, who obviously didn't know, ruin his day. We should all have the boldness and confidence of a lion.

Conclusion

So who are you, really? How do you finish the statement, I AM _____?

If you still don't know, did you take the Personality Profile test at www.personalityinsights.com or www.thedelspersonalitytest.com? It is worth the effort and investment in yourself. Spend some time, right now, to really think about who you are. As you think about it, try thinking in the way that works best for you. My solution is to go to a very quiet room with no distractions and just meditate. Maybe you need to pace back and forth. Maybe you need to listen to some music. Maybe you just need to push the talk button, and keep talking until something brilliant comes out of your mouth. I am sure you know yourself well enough to know which of these ways works best for you. Now you know why. It is because your brain is wired to think that way. And you probably just thought you were weird!

I will tell you that you are much more unique that you can imagine. No one has your DNA. Your personality is unique. The way you think is unique. Your experiences and your memories are unique. All of these combine to make you who you really are. The really great thing about your uniqueness is that your Father created you to be just like you are. That doesn't mean He doesn't want you to improve, but He made you like this for a reason, and He loves you for who He made you to be. He does not compare you to anyone else, because there is no comparison. All of the parts of what makes you so unique were given to you: you did nothing to earn them. What are you going to do with your uniqueness?

Part III

The Second Question

Chapter 12

The Second Question

You have a seed of greatness in you. Notice that was a statement, not a question. It is a fact that each one us has a particular gift that, when developed, can enable us to be recognized as geniuses. By gift, I mean you have a natural talent or ability that really sets you apart. The problem is that most of us don't know what it is. An even sadder fact is that most people aren't even looking for it. Why is that?

The Second question of *The Holy Hand Grenade* is, **What is your gift?** If you knew you had a special gift you were great at, and it could take you as far as you wanted to go in life, wouldn't you want to know what it is? Yet the fear of discovering just how great you can really be is overwhelming to many. It is much easier to go through life without knowing how great you can be. Then, no one will expect anything of you, including yourself. Ultimately, I guess you could call this the fear of success. The quote I think most completely addresses our fear of success actually comes from the Bible.

"You are the light of the world. A city set on a hill cannot be hidden; nor does anyone light a lamp and put it under a basket, but on the lamp stand, and it gives light to all who are in the house. Let your light shine before men in such a way that they may see your good works, and glorify your Father who is in heaven. [20]"

If Jesus were here to tell you what this means, I imagine it would be something like this:

> *"You, **yes you**, are the light of the world. The gift in you shines for all the world to see. You have been blessed with a gift to be a blessing. But, if you keep that light, that gift, to yourself, and hide it from view, how will it give light to those around you who need your light in order to see. Others need your light in order to see their way. Why would you cover up this marvelous gift from God? Are you afraid what someone might say about you? So what if they say, 'Look at you, who do you think you are?' Don't you know that whatever, or whomever you fear, fears God? He is the one you should be concerned about pleasing. Without your light, the very ones who criticize you might stumble and fall. How many will stay in darkness because you are afraid of what someone else says about your light shining?*
>
> *But you think, 'I don't have a gift; there is no light in me that can shine for others.' Have you looked? I mean REALLY looked? Or did you just assume that something that great could not possibly be in you? Do you not know that your Father loves you so much that He has put something special, something unique inside of you? You know this is true, don't you? You already know you are different. You know your DNA is different from anyone else in the world, and so are your fingerprints. You subconsciously hide your gift, your light, because you don't think it is as great as someone else's gift. You may also hide your gift because you are afraid of how it might change your life. If you don't stop hiding your light, you will never know the awesome life you were intended to live.*
>
> *Trust Him. Trust that your Father knew exactly what He was*

---

20 *The Holy Bible*, Matthew 5:14-16

doing when He graced you with His marvelous light. Trust Him more than anyone who could level criticism against you. It is worth the effort. It is how you will make a difference.

When you have the courage to let your light shine, it gives courage to others who also need to let their lights shine. You have been graced, not just with the gift that is your light, but also with all of the courage you need for your light to shine as brightly as it can shine. When you use that grace, and don't set it aside on the table, it greatly pleases your Father. He gave you your gift, the grace to use it, and His courage to shine before men to show them how good He is. You are the light of the world, not for your glory, but for His. His promise to you is that when you put His glory as your first priority, He will take care of all your needs, and so much more. He is able to do exceedingly above anything you could ever ask or imagine, and He gave you the key to His abundance. Will you use it? He has other gifts for you, as well. Do you want them? All you have to do is ask.

You are the light of the world. Let it shine!"

Our biggest fear is not that we are inadequate. Almost everyone I know feels inadequate, somehow. Don't you? I have had many more people tell me what I couldn't do, than what I could do. Haven't you, too? I had a dream to play professional baseball at one time. The problem was my fastball wasn't all that fast. I felt inadequate, and no one argued with me. When I decided to leave the Marine Corps and go into the business world, my own mother told me repeatedly that I couldn't do that, and I wasn't a businessman. And dating!!! How many opportunities did you miss because you felt inadequate? I can't count mine. I'm glad I asked Mary out (actually, I dared her to go out with me) and overcame my feelings of inadequacy. After we were engaged, she laughingly told me one of our mutual acquaintances had asked her, "Who would marry Tom Gilroy?" Now, that's a real morale booster.

Actually, our greatest fear is to find out just how powerful we truly are. That is pretty much what I am telling you when I say you have a seed of greatness in you, and there is a gift in you so wonderful that once you have developed it, you will be thought of as a genius. I did not begin to understand this kind of fear until I realized who my Daddy is. When you get a grip on who your Father really is, then the idea that you can be powerful beyond measure can actually become a reality to you. Once you realize you are literally a child of God, and not just in a figurative sense, then that makes you a prince or princess of the King of Kings. If you are just some Joe Shmoe, then you may have a point in asking, "Who am I to be brilliant, beautiful, talented, and a genius." But you aren't just Joe Shmoe. Saint Paul was telling the same thing to the Romans when he told them, "For you have not received a spirit of slavery, leading to fear again, but you have received a spirit of adoption as sons by which we cry out, 'Abba!' Father. The Spirit Himself testifies with our spirit that we are children of God, and if children, heirs also, heirs of God and fellow heirs with Christ.[21]"

If you are an heir of God, and all He has to give, and you are His Prince or Princess, doesn't it follow that you actually could be brilliant, beautiful, talented, and a genius. I mean it would be possible, right? Once I began to understand that this was actually true and could apply to me, just as it applies to you, that is when I really got scared. Not only did Jesus say, "You are the light of the world," but He also said, "The works that I do, you will do also; and greater works than these will you do.[22]" If that is true (and it is), doesn't it frighten you just a tad? If you are that good, and brilliant, aren't you going to stick out just a little? Aren't people going to ask you just who you think you are?

If you are a child of God, then there is nothing humble about shrinking back to your old self that doesn't stick out just so other people won't feel insecure around you. You were born to manifest the glory of God that He gave you as a gift. If you don't do it, you are slapping Him in the face, telling Him, "No, you can keep your gift, I just want to be mediocre." And your gift, the way you let your light shine, is unique to you, but everyone has a gift just as unique. Each person has a gift just as wonderful. They are probably just as scared as you are to let it out. So, as you let your light shine, you allow others to gather the courage to let their lights shine. As

---

21 *The Holy Bible*, Romans 8:15-17

22 *The Holy Bible*, John 14:12

you overcome your fear of the greatness in you and begin to let it out, you actually have a part in liberating someone else from a mediocre life to the abundant life that God has for them.

Your *acting* meek doesn't serve the world: *being* meek does. Meekness lies in knowing your gift was given to you, and that you must in turn give it to others. When I ask people what they really want to do, almost all of them reply they don't know. But what they do know is that they want to make a difference somehow. They want to know they have something of value they can contribute, for which they are valued and appreciated. Isn't that how you feel?

The problem is you can't play small and still be significant at the same time. If you have something in you that is brilliant, and for which you are recognized as being great, then having a false sense of humility so you won't stick out in a crowd doesn't help anything. Real humility is using your gift to its fullest potential, so the maximum number of people can benefit from it. You won't need to seek recognition, because you will naturally be recognized for your gift. If you still feel the need to seek recognition, then you are probably not operating in a God-given gift.

Have you ever held back your talent so that you didn't overshadow someone else? If so, why did you do it? Was it to make the other person feel better? If so, how many people benefited from your holding back? How many more would have been blessed if you had let your light shine instead. I think all of us can relate to the feeling of holding back in order to not upset the apple cart at some time or other. The question is why? Sometimes it is because we are not confident in our gifts. Sometimes we are afraid of offending people if we overshadow them. Sometimes this fear is so great we don't even look for what we do well, or seek the gift we have been blessed with.

In James Allen's book *As A Man Thinketh,* he writes, "The will to do comes from the knowledge that we can do.[23]" So, where do we get the knowledge that we can do something so well, and with such passion, that we are recognized as geniuses at it? The first clue comes from your personality. As we have already discussed, your personality was given to you for a very specific reason, and it suits you perfectly. You have other attributes that complement your personality as well.

---

23   *As A Man Thinketh*, James Allen

Chapter 13

Security versus Freedom

I recently watched a National Geographic special that looked into why some cultures advanced faster than others. The conclusion they drew is that cultures advanced when their regions of the world had cultivated a food source that was more abundant than the needs of the population. This allowed people to specialize in different areas of trade, rather than everyone having to be involved in hunting, gathering, or farming for survival. In other words, once a culture could get out of the survival mode, specialization occurred, and that culture took off.

Believe it or not, the same is true for you today. Many people today are stuck in a survival mode. Their only thought is making enough money for food, shelter, and security. Those people want someone, almost anyone, to provide security for them so they can go on surviving. That someone could be their boss, their union, or the government. As long as the boss, the union, or the government is in control of providing the security for their survival, people will not be engaged in seeking their gifts and finding out how special they are. That is because in survival, everyone has to be engaged in just surviving.

If you are in the survival mode right now, pay attention, because you don't have to stay there. I have a question for you. If you depend on your boss, a union, the government, or anyone else for your security and survival, wouldn't you admit that those who provide your security have broken out of the need for security themselves? Their survival no longer depends on their own production, but on yours, right? But, what happens to them if you decide to break out of the mold and no longer depend on them? Do they like that, and encourage it? Probably not, since their abundance depends on you staying in survival mode.

This is an interesting situation that many Americans and other citizens of the "free world" find themselves in. We say we live in a free country, but many have freely given their freedom to someone else in exchange for security. Our laws and constitution protect our rights, but they do not prevent a person's free will from choosing to place their freedom in someone else's hands.

I have personally experienced how difficult it is to pursue your gift when you have a hard time paying your bills. The stress and pressure to do anything just to "get by" can be oppressive. When someone comes along and says he will help you keep your job, pay your bills, or give you a loan for a house, it looks like a present from heaven. But is it? Instead, how much more fulfilling would it be if you could develop and use your gift to get these things? It matters in whom you place your trust. The person, or entity, in whom you place your trust, will end up becoming your master. Do you trust in the government; do you trust in your company; do you trust in your spouse; do you trust in yourself; or do you trust in God?

In order to determine who your master is, you have to ask yourself a couple of questions. Do you really want your freedom, or are you OK with giving it to someone else? If you want your freedom, but you are currently in survival mode, how do you get out? What do you have an abundance of (more than you need to survive) right now? As you take inventory of your situation, your quick answer may be NOTHING! But is that really true? While you may not have enough money, do you have any extra time? In the end, time is worth much more than money.

How are you using your time? Are you wasting it watching TV or on the Internet? Or are you using it to produce more? While I am not suggesting you quit the job that is helping you to survive right now, most of you have at least some time that could be devoted to self-improvement. As I write this book, that is exactly what I am doing. I have a business in which I get to use my talents. My business pays the bills and provides some extras, but my passion and my gift are developed in my spare time. Some may say it is too much work, but for me it is exciting and what I know I am supposed to do.

Taking that step, and investing your time into your gift is what will take you from survival mode to abundance. It will lift you from being a number at a job to someone who has a gift that is in demand. It will take you from feeling like you are a nobody to feeling like the special somebody that you really are.

Chapter 14

Talent

The word *talent* can mean different things to different people. In fact, there are several definitions in the dictionary. So, providing my definition for *talent* will help to clear up some potential confusion. Some people use the words *skill, ability,* or *aptitude* interchangeably with the word *talent*. We need to be more specific in order for the next section to make sense.

Skilled Versus Talented

When you use the word *skill,* it means that you have the ability to use your knowledge effectively. So, skills are learned. As a Marine, I had to work extremely hard to be a good pilot. I was enamored with the image of being a pilot, and the respect and admiration that went along with it. But almost every mission I flew was very hard work for me. I came back from most missions drenched in sweat, and physically and mentally exhausted. On the same missions I flew, there were other pilots who came back completely exhilarated. I had to work my butt off while they were having fun. That is because they were naturally talented, where I was skilled. My abilities were all learned, while theirs were natural.

Ability

When you use the word *ability*, it means you have the quality or state of being able. So, if you have the ability to do something, it means you can do it; that it is possible. However, just because you have the ability to do something doesn't mean you like doing it. How many times have you heard teachers explain to parents that they don't understand why their children don't get better grades. After all, they have the ability! Or how often do we see athletes who have abilities well beyond their performances. So, you might be able to do something, but ability, by itself, is no true indicator of success.

Aptitude

When you use the word *aptitude*, it means we have the capacity for learning something. So, if you have the aptitude for something, you have the ability to learn about it, and it makes sense to you. One of the most common tests that school guidance counselors and career placement professionals use is some form of an aptitude test. Sometimes, they call these personality tests, but they are heavily skewed in the direction of available career fields, and are not really personality tests. These tests attempt to measure your aptitude for doing certain kinds of work. You may have an aptitude for mechanical work, but have no desire for that kind of career. You may have an aptitude for learning languages, but a career as an interpreter seems very boring to you. My all-time favorite is this: you may have an aptitude for being an accountant, with the almost guarantee of always having a job, but the idea of doing accounting as a career doesn't appeal to you at all.

Talent

The word talent means having skills, abilities, aptitudes and something more. The word *talent* comes from the Greek word *talanton*. A *talanton* was a scale or a balance used for measuring the mass of things. The Greeks and the Romans referred to a *talent* as a measure of gold or silver; and by the time the New Testament was written, a talent was equal to 58.9 kilograms. A talent of silver, as described in Matthew's Gospel, was worth about fifteen years wages. Another way to describe a talent is as a unit of value. So, while we can say someone's talent may be a skill, ability, or an aptitude, if it cannot be converted it into something of value, like silver or gold, then it is not a talent. **Talent is a natural (not learned) ability that has value.**

In the book of Matthew, there is a parable about talents. The point of the parable was not about how much talent one has, but about what you do with what you have been given. It matters very much that you make the best use of what you have been given. According to this parable, being afraid to use your talent is not a good thing. Even if you have read or heard the parable of the talents a hundred times, it would be worth revisiting, in light of equating talents with your gift. You can find it in Matthew, chapter 25.[24]

Spiritual Money

The best book I have read on the subject of finding one's gift is Robert Kiyosaki's *Before you Quit Your Job*[25]. I know it may seem an unlikely source, but in the middle of the book, Kiyosaki has a discussion with his "Rich Dad" about the three kinds of money. I encourage you to read the book for yourself, but I will paraphrase the parts that relate to finding your gift. Kiyosaki says there are three kinds of money:

- » Competitive money
- » Cooperative money
- » Spiritual money

Competitive money is what most people work for, and it involves competing against others. Cooperative money involves teamwork with others, and cooperating, rather than competing. The third and highest kind of money is what he calls spiritual money. This is money created in response to a higher calling; work that God wants done.

---

24 *The Holy Bible*, Matthew 25:14-30
25 *Before You Quit Your Job, 10 Real-Life Lessons Every Entrepreneur Should Know About Building a Multimillion-Dollar Business*, Robert T. Kiyosaki with Sharon L. Lechter, CPA

While he calls it spiritual money, it really isn't about money. "It's about doing a job not because you want to do it but because it must be done, and you know down deep in your soul that you're the one who is supposed to do it." Kiyosaki goes on to say that if you were truly committed to solving the problem, the invisible forces of the universe, of God, might come to your support. Magic might happen in your life. This is when spiritual money comes into play. But it is more than money. People you never met before come to join forces with you—not for the money, but for the mission. One of the keys to attracting the invisible spiritual forces is to be dedicated to giving your gift. Your gift is "a special God-given talent. Something you are the best at. A talent God gave especially to you."

The Second Question of *The Holy Hand Grenade,* is **What is your Gift?** This is the perfect place to properly define gift. Please recall that the real you is made of spirit, soul, and body. The gift I am speaking of here is part of your soul (which is made of your mind, will and emotions). As a Christian, I believe we also have spiritual gifts, but I am not addressing them at this point, except to say your spiritual gift and your natural gift will always work together.

Your gift is a natural talent you possess. You may actually have several natural talents. Having several talents can be a good thing, but it has the bad habit of confusing people who are seeking their gift because they can do several things well. Your **gift** is the one talent that:

» Stands out above the rest
» Can be developed to greatness
» You find fulfilling
» You would be willing to dedicate your life to

Finding your Gift;
the one talent that stands out above the rest.

So now, the $64 million question: How do you find this God-given talent, your gift? Aren't you wondering that? You already have the first piece of the answer. Part of the answer is in your personality. Remember your personality is another God-given gift. He predisposed you to think and behave in a certain way, on purpose.

The next step is to discover the particular talent you are the best at. Tom Rath, author of *StrengthsFinder 2.0* [26], calls the talents that you do best your "Strengths." According to Rath, "What StrengthsFinder actually measures is talent, not strength." So even a bestselling author, and the organization that conducted countless interviews regarding this information, have some terminology issues. To keep things simple, I will refer to the top talent, or strength that you do the best, as your **gift**.

If you purchase the book *Strengthsfinder2.0*, which I highly recommend, you will find a code number in the back of the book that will enable you to take an online strengths test. When you buy the book, the online test is free. The test will identify your top five strengths. These are the talents you do best. I have found this test to be invaluable. Most people, me included, are either unaware of their talents, or unable to describe them in a way that can be translated into anything useful. How important do you think it would be to find out the top God-given talent you possess—your gift?

When I took the *StrenthsFinders 2.0* test, I was surprised at how accurate it was. I had an idea of what my talents were, but there is no way I could articulate them so they would make sense to someone else. I also didn't know what my top talent (gift) was, how it compared to other talents, and how it related to my personality. What you will find is that your gift lines up perfectly with your personality. Without the right personality, your gift could not be used effectively.

If you are like me, you will be amazed at how much your gift (the top strength/talent in the profile you receive from the *StrengthsFinder 2.0* test) is a natural part of who you are. The challenge you may face is that the gift it describes may not be the magic revelation you hoped for. Your reaction might be something like "Yeah, that describes me, and, yes, I feel like that pretty often, but it's no big deal." Actually, it is very big deal.

If you have taken the test, and you have found out what your gift is, do you think everyone has that gift? Let me help you with that…NO! Especially if you combine your gift with the other major talents you possess and your personality. Pay very close attention to the **Ideas for Action** listed for your gift. Does one of these ideas jump out at you? This is the kind of stuff you just can't read once and think you got it. You have to meditate

---

26 *Strengthsfinder 2.0*, Tom Rath

on this information. Give it some real thought and effort. Talk it over with the mentor in your life and get some help to make sense of it all.

The all-time greatest self-help book was written by Napoleon Hill, and is on the reading list of almost all CEOs. The name of the book is *Think and Grow Rich*[27]. People read the entire book and don't find the secret to getting what they want out of life. That amazes me, because the secret is on the cover. If you want to be rich (in money, love, relationships, etc.) you have to THINK! No one can do that for you.

As James Allen says, "The aphorism 'As a man thinketh in his heart so is he' not only embraces the whole of man's being but is so comprehensive as to reach out to every condition and circumstance of his life. **A man is literally what he thinks**, his character being the complete sum of all his thoughts.[28]"

According to the research that Rath did in conjunction with the Gallup organization, after surveying more than ten million people worldwide, they found people who had the opportunity to focus on their strengths—as opposed to managing their weaknesses—were three times more likely to have an excellent quality of life, in general, and six times more likely to be engaged in their jobs. The premise of his book is this: in order to do great things in life, one must focus on his or her strengths. I agree with him, but I don't think that goes far enough. I think that in order to have a fulfilled and happy life, you need to find the one thing for which you were created.

Every person whom the world views as great had one thing in common: they were focused on what they were exceptional at doing. Emerson called it finding your best self. Napoleon Hill called it finding your purpose and a definite chief aim. The description I like the best goes like this:

Not that I have already obtained it or have become perfect, but I press on so that I may lay hold of that for which also I was laid hold of by Christ Jesus. Brethren, I do not regard myself as having laid hold of it yet; but one thing I do: forgetting what lies behind and reaching forward to what

---

27 *Think and Grow Rich*, Napoleon Hill

28 *As a Man Thinketh*, James Allen

lies ahead, I press on toward the goal for the prize of the upward call of God in Christ Jesus.[29]

Please allow me to explain how I interpret this passage from Paul's letter to the Philippians. Paul was a stubborn, hardheaded, and well-educated Jew, whose mission was to take the message of Jesus to non-Jews. Many regarded him as arrogant and argumentative, but he knew he was the right man for the job. He was so mission-oriented that he would not rest until the entire known world had been exposed to his teaching. So, when he wrote the above passage to the Philippians, he knew he had not fulfilled his calling yet, but he was still pursuing it. He knew the one thing he was supposed to do, and it gave him laser-like focus. He did not look backwards on past failures, his weaknesses, or even his successes. He was entirely forward oriented. But note what the reason was: there was a prize at the end of his pursuit, and that is what he was going after. He was absolutely sure of his mission, that he was uniquely suited to accomplish it, and that there was a reward awaiting him when it was accomplished. This is exactly what you should expect as well.

You are chosen

An interesting aspect of finding your gift is that you were chosen for it. You do not choose your gift; it was chosen for you. This way of thinking can rub us Americans the wrong way, so let me explain.

If you were raised in the United States, you may have been brought up to believe in self-determination and that you are the captain of your own fate. To some degree, that is true. You do have the ability to choose, and you can say "no" to things you don't want to do. Our Declaration of Independence states that we have been endowed by our Creator with certain unalienable Rights, that among these are Life, Liberty and the pursuit of Happiness. As a republic, we have more liberty to choose our destinies than most countries. Even so, to say you can do anything that you put your mind to is not entirely correct.

You have to work within the talents and attributes you posses. If you are five feet tall, have white man's disease (no vertical jump), and you can't

---

29 *The Holy Bible*, Philippians 3:12-14

shoot, your chances of being an NBA superstar are remote, no matter how much you want it. Your physical size, your personality, and your talent are gifts you were born with. Your choice involves using them and developing them. You cannot choose to be six feet tall if your mature height is five feet. You cannot choose to be a great singer if you were born tone deaf. In the United States, you have the liberty to pursue things, even if you have no gifts in those areas—but that does not mean you will be successful.

My point is this: you have very special talents and attributes for a reason. The sooner you accept those talents and attributes, and begin developing them, rather than wishing for talents and attributes that are not yours, the sooner you will discover your real gift. The sooner you develop your gift, that one talent you do best, the sooner you will fulfill your quest.

My personal source for truth comes from Jesus. If there are books that can teach me things, that is great, but they must line up with Scripture or else they are suspect to me. Here is what Jesus said: "You did not choose Me but I chose you, and appointed you that you would go and bear fruit, and that your fruit would remain…[30]"

Suppose you live in a kingdom, not a democracy or republic, and the king summons you. When you come before him, he tells you that you were specifically chosen for an important mission. How would that make you feel? Wouldn't you feel special, especially if the king had many other people to choose from, but he chose you? Now, what if the king also told you he thought you had all the right attributes to accomplish the mission, and that he had complete confidence in you? Now, how would you feel?

That is what Jesus is saying. He does not operate in a democracy. God's way is a kingdom. In the kingdoms of old, the king or his ministers chose people for tasks and gave them the means to carry them out. It is the same with your gift. You have been given a gift and you have been chosen for a mission. Your mission (or task, or purpose, or definite chief aim) is to bear fruit that remains. When you do this, you will be truly happy. So even though our government does not have a king, the rights to life, liberty, and the pursuit of happiness, as written in the Declaration of Independence, enable us to carry out our mission and use our gift as no other country allows.

---

30 The Holy Bible, John 15:16

Chapter 15

Comparison

One of the things that cause people not to recognize or develop their gifts is comparison.

The dictionary says when we *compare*, we are examining the character or qualities of a thing in order to discover resemblances or differences. Comparison infers that you are examining something to determine if it has more value than something else.

If you compare your gift to someone else's gift, you may perceive that one gift is better than another. There are two dangers here. First, if you think your gift is superior to that of someone else, you may think you are superior to that person. Feeling superior to others causes all kinds of problems in the world today. It is the source of racial tensions, of wars, and of all manner of disputes.

On the other hand, if you think someone else's gift is superior to yours, you may feel inferior to that person. If you think your gift is inferior to someone else's, you may think you are inferior. If you feel inferior, you may be willing to accept less out of life than you have a right to. If you feel inferior, you may think the only way to get what you want is to take it from someone else who has more. None of this is based on the truth.

Our Constitution is based on the premise that all men are created equal. Our laws, society, and way of life are built on that premise. When things get out of whack in the United States, most of the time it is because one group of people feels superior, and another group feels inferior. Our system of government, based on the law, is supposed to protect everyone equally in order to prevent just such problems.

Saint Paul recognized this issue. To the early Christian church, he wrote the following messages about gifts and how we are supposed to use them. His instructions are equally relevant today, and apply both inside and outside the church. He was acutely aware of how divisive comparison can be. He was also keenly aware of how powerful gifts can be, if they are used in unity for one purpose. The analogy he used to get his message across concerns how the human body functions. The following quotes from the Bible are a little long, and Paul is addressing spiritual gifts, but please read through them carefully; there is a good reason.

The first quote comes from Paul when he was in Corinth and writing to new Christians in Rome. Some of these new Christians were former pagans, and some were Jews. They had very diverse backgrounds and Paul was teaching them some radical things. By the time we get to chapter 12 of the book of Romans, he has already told them that they have salvation (eternal life with God) and righteousness (being able to stand in God's presence with no condemnation) as free gifts because of what Jesus had done for them. This was radical indeed, since they all believed that following an impossibly strict code of laws (or the whims of the "gods") was what made them or broke them in the afterlife. So, in chapter 12 he begins to introduce other gifts.

> *"For through the grace (unmerited favor of God) given to me I say to everyone among you not to think more highly of himself than he ought to think; but to think so as to have sound judgment, as God has allotted to each a measure of faith. For just as we have many members (organs, parts) in one body and all the members do not have the same function, so we, who are many, are one body in Christ, and individually members one of another. Since we have gifts*

that differ according to the grace given to us, each of us is to exercise them accordingly.[31]*"*

Paul tells us not to think higher about ourselves than we ought to. Notice that he did not say to feel bad about yourself. Just as a human body has many parts, but all belong and function as one body, so should the people he is talking to. They may have different gifts, but they are all supposed to work together, and one gift is not higher than another.

The next quote comes from Paul talking to the new Christians in Corinth. Corinth was like an old world Las Vegas. The Corinthian Christians he is talking to in this letter were mostly from pagan religions and still practiced all kinds of pagan immorality, also like Las Vegas. However, the Corinthian church was growing like wildfire. The message that salvation and righteousness were free gifts from God, rather than things that could be earned, really penetrated these folks.

> *"Now there are varieties of gifts, but the same Spirit. And there are varieties of ministries, and the same Lord. There are varieties of effects, but the same God who works all things in all persons. But to each one is given the manifestation of the Spirit for the common good.*
>
> *For the body is not one member, but many. If the foot says, 'Because I am not a hand, I am not part of the body,' it is not for this reason any less a part of the body. And if the ear says, 'Because I am not an eye, I am not a part of the body,' it is not for this reason any less a part of the body. If the whole body were an eye, where would the hearing be? If the whole were hearing, where would the sense of smell be?* **But God has placed the members, each one of them, in the body, just as He desired.**
>
> *If they were all one member, where would the body be? But now there are many members, but one body. And the eye cannot say to the hand, 'I have no need of you;' or again the*

---

31 *The Holy Bible*, Romans 12:3-6

> *head to the feet, 'I have no need of you.' On the contrary, it is much truer that the members of the body which seem to be weaker are necessary; and those members of the body which we deem less honorable, on these we bestow more abundant honor, and our less presentable members become much more presentable, whereas our more presentable members have no need of it. But God has so composed the body, giving more abundant honor to that member which lacked, so that there may be no division in the body, but that the members may have the same care one for another. And if one member suffers, all the members suffer with it; if one member is honored, all the members rejoice with it.[32]"*

Paul is telling the Corinthians, and you, that God gave you a gift and placed you in the body, exactly as He desired. Since His desire is for you to have an abundant life, then that gift is your ticket to the big-time. Paul also cautions that one member, and his gift, is not to be more highly esteemed than another. Your gift is extremely important if the body is going to work the way it is supposed to.

Unfortunately, the body is not working too well right now. I believe that is because most people do not know what their gifts are. The few that do know their gift (whether natural or spiritual) don't know how to work with others in the body. Many times, the one who knows his or her gift thinks that it is the most important part of the body, and may exclude other functions that are just as important. The result is that the body doesn't function as properly as it should. This is just as true for businesses, and other organizations as it is for a church. The point is this: your membership and proper functioning in the body isn't just important for you, but to everyone else, as well.

Ephesus was the most important city in Western Asia Minor (now called Turkey) because it was a huge commercial center. Paul made Ephesus the center of his mission for several years. In his letter to the Ephesians, he isn't correcting them for anything this time, which was unusual for Paul.

---

32 *The Holy Bible*, 1 Corinthians, 12:7, 14-28

He carries on the theme of the Body of Christ with them in chapter four, but carries it further, talking about how to act mature.

> *"And He (Jesus) gave some as apostles, and some as prophets, and some as evangelists, and some as pastors and teachers, for the equipping of the saints for the work of service, to the building up of the body of Christ; until we all attain to the unity of the faith, and the knowledge of the Son of God, to a mature man, to the measure and stature which belongs to the fullness of Christ.*
>
> *As a result, we are no longer to be children, tossed here and there by waves and carried about by every wind of doctrine, by the trickery of men, by craftiness in deceitful scheming; but speaking the truth in love, we are to grow up in all aspects into Him who is the head, even Christ, from whom the whole body, being fitted together by what every joint supplies, according to the proper working of each individual part, causes the growth of the body for the building up of itself in love.[33]"*

Notice that Paul says there are offices that many hold in greater esteem, whose purpose it is to prepare the folks who are going to do the work. In God's kingdom, one person's gift is not better than another person's. After all, He gave us the gifts. All we do is receive them and use them. The result of realizing your gift, and using it properly, is that you will become more mature.

The people Paul was describing as being crafty, deceitful, and scheming were Christians inside the church. Unfortunately, the situation hasn't improved much in the 2000 years since Paul wrote this. When Christians, today, refer to the Body of Christ, they almost universally use it as a synonym for the Church (Church, with an uppercase "C" meaning all people that call themselves Christian; while church with a lowercase "c", meaning a local group of believers). That is not what Paul had in mind in the above passages. There is more jealousy inside the Church than outside

---

33 *The Holy Bible*, Ephesians 4:11-16

the Church, and that jealousy is the result of comparison. It is no wonder so many people are turned off by religion, today.

But he did nail the problem. When each one of us knows our gift, where we fit in, and we are working properly, then we will no longer be tossed here and there. Then we will see the building up of the Body of Christ in love that Paul describes. That is the goal. Unfortunately, it does not exist yet. When you realize that your gift and your appointment came from the King, why would you be jealous of anyone else? Knowing who you are and how you fit into the body, you should have no need or desire for comparison.

Chapter 16

Developing Your Gift

It is not enough to just know you have a gift. And it is not enough just to know what that gift is. In order to be great, you have to use your gift; and in order to use your gift effectively, you first have to develop it.

Anyone who is recognized at being truly gifted has had to go through the hard work to develop that gift. Whether the gifted person is an athlete, a musician, a motivational speaker, a writer, an attorney, or a salesman, he has to perfect his craft in order to become great at it. Even though it is hard work, the one who develops his gift does it as a labor of love. He is the one practicing when the rest of the team has gone home. He is the one doing scales and vocal training when no one is listening, and he is the one making extra sales calls when no one else would dream of it. Gifted people put in the extra effort, not because they have to, but because they want to. They love what they do and they want to be the best at it.

My mother was a competitive figure skater in Germany and turned professional at twenty-four years old. She told me stories of practicing ice skating in meat lockers, as a little girl, because there was nowhere else to go in post World War II East Germany. She later became a coach in Northern Virginia, and she would tell me of being on the ice with her students at four in the morning to help them prepare for their next skating test. While I thought she was nuts, she thought it was all part of what it took to be a great skater. She loved it, and her skaters loved her.

Have you ever known a musician? Have you noticed he or she is always doing something with, or about music? It could be practicing, checking out someone else's technique, or talking with other musicians, but a good musician is always engaged in music. The musician speaks a whole different language, and even their thoughts are musical.

How about computer geeks? Not everyone can be a great athlete or musician, but most of us have run into someone who just thinks like a computer. Such people intuitively understand how networks work, how code is written, and how to solve huge business problems by using computers and developing software. To me, computers are a necessary part of life today, but they are usually more infuriating than a source of enjoyment. Self-proclaimed "computer geeks" habitually study computer hardware; software being their passion. A computer geek never seems to talk about anything else.

I worked with a young lady who was absolutely gifted at tracking data. She could use every facet of what Microsoft had developed to track even the smallest of details. Her presentation of data wasn't just on spread sheets, but on bar graphs, colored pie charts, and any other way the data could be presented so it would make sense. She did her work at the office, at home, on vacation…it didn't seem to matter to her. The thought of me having to do it was a nightmare, but she really loved it. I certainly appreciated her phenomenal work.

So, while developing your gift may look like herculean effort to someone else, to you it is part of what you do. You enjoy the hard work because the reward for using your gift makes it all worthwhile. Sometimes the reward is just in the knowing that there is no one as good as you are at what you do.

Chapter 17

Resistance

In Robert Kiyosaki's book *Before you Quit Your Job,* he talks about resistance. Resistance is a force that tries to hold you back. Sometimes, we feel resistance in the form of procrastination. You know, the feeling that comes over you every time you think it is time to get it in gear—but not until tomorrow. It is amazing how tomorrow can end up being years instead of just a day. Or resistance can come from some well-meaning friends or relatives who just don't want you to get your hopes up too high. Right! Their resistance may be aimed at you, but it could also be their own resistance justifying their current condition, when deep down inside, they know better.

Resistance isn't just a force that wants to hold us back for no reason. Resistance wants to keep us from "turning pro". Kiyosaki has an interesting view of the difference between being an amateur and being a professional. Most people think that an amateur plays a sport for the "love of the game," while a professional just does it for the money. He makes the case that it is the professional who really loves the sport. He loves it so much he has dedicated himself completely to it. While the amateur plays part-time, the professional is full time. The game is an avocation to the amateur, but for the professional, it is his vocation. He is committed!

Resistance hates it when we decide to commit. It seems as if all hell is unleashed when we decide to really commit to using our gifts. In a way, that is not at all that far from the truth. If you really committed yourself to developing your gift to the point where you are a recognized professional, how many people could you affect? Ten? Ten thousand? Ten million? If you don't develop your gift and use it, how many people will you affect? If you were the Devil, would you want a bunch of people walking around committed to using their God-given gifts, or would you try to stop them? Judging by the lack of commitment I see in the world, I'd say the Devil has done a pretty good job, so far. The good news is that just a few committed people dedicated to using their gifts can make an amazing impact. It only takes a few to let their light shine in order to give others permission to shine as well.

Paradigm shifts and Resistance

In addition to the internal resistance we all have to face if we want to use our gift, there is also external resistance. The external resistance comes from many places, but I think it comes primarily from a paradigm shift. There is more change occurring in the world now, and at a faster rate, than in any time in history. The last time a change of this magnitude occurred, we called it the Industrial Revolution. That was when the populations of the civilized world made the leap from being agriculturally centered economies to industrialized based economies.

Industrial Revolution 101

Millions of people all over the world had their universe turned upside down because of the industrial revolution. The economic system of agriculturally centered society had evolved for thousands of years. There were wealthy landowners, poor land working serfs or slaves, and a middle class of merchants and small farm owners. Land was the most prized possession. Most wars were fought by kings who wanted to take away lands from other kings in order to gain wealth. Almost all trade was based on something that was grown, whether it was coffee, tea, sugar, silk, cotton, or grain, and all of these valued commodities somehow came from the land.

Likewise, most peoples' professions and identities came from how they fit into this agriculturally centered society. Kings ruled the country (with the U.S. being the only notable exception), and the population served the king and his land-owning aristocracy. The chances of escaping your position in society were minimal, and were largely determined by your ability to gain control of some land for yourself. All of this radically changed with the advent of the Industrial Revolution.

Seemingly overnight, in the course of 100 years or less, the economy of the major nations became more reliant on what could be produced through industry, rather than through agriculture. In the agricultural age, what was valued most was having a surplus of food. Once there was enough food, people could specialize in building, creating and selling luxuries, and the arts. During the Industrial Age, machines could do the farming work of many people, so less value was placed on food needs, and more value was put on machines that could do the work instead of people. Large populations of farmers and field hands were put out of work. A mass migration from rural areas to cities occurred, and people's identities changed. Independent thinking and resourcefulness were valued assets for farming communities, but in the industrial centers of the early steel mills and automobile factories, your value was based on doing the same thing over and over again in a predetermined fashion. People became replaceable parts of a factory. Now, the captains of industry became the wealthy, replacing the aristocracy. Wars were fought over natural resources of rubber, oil, and iron ore, in order to keep machines and industry going. A country's ability to manufacture products was what created its wealth. This led to the imperialistic colonization of nations, and why "the war to end all wars" was regarded as the First World War. A mainly European war was carried over into all of their colonies, leaving no one unscathed. Since the First World War was never really resolved, it led to the Second World War. In the post World War II era, the U.S. emerged as the industrial powerhouse because it was the only world power that did not have to rebuild itself. The American Dream—owning a home and having an automobile in every driveway—was birthed in this era, and became the standard. As American industrial dominance grew, so did the affluence of the average American. It was also during this time that the myth (a supposed fact at the time) began that American managerial skills and leadership could dominate any and all situations.

> **Industrial Age**
>
> » 1880-1989 Golden Age of U.S. Industry
>
> In some ways the Civil War was a precursor to the turmoil of the coming change from Agriculture to Industry. The Industrial North was able to defeat the Agricultural South. With the advent of inexpensively produced steel, American Industry grew quickly and continued into the 1980s.
>
> » 1945-1979 American Dream
>
> The "American Dream" of every family with a house and a car in the driveway came from the post WWII industrial era. Unprecedented growth and wealth as a result of America's industrial prowess blessed most American families.
>
> » 1970-1989 Transition—industry to Third World
>
> A gradual shift from U.S. manufacturing plants to globalization of manufacturing began to take place. With globalization came increased pressure to keep costs lower in order to compete with other countries.

Information Age

In the post-World War II era, the only real rival to American economic and industrial power in the world came from the Soviet Union. A new type of conflict emerged—the "Cold War." The Cold War involved a jockeying for control of first place as THE industrial, economic, and nuclear power of the world. It was also the conflict of two very different ideologies, and it served to jumpstart the next major shift in world power. While the advent of the industrial revolution changed the world at a tremendous pace never before imagined, the next change would dwarf it in size and speed.

The Information Age was ushered in as a result of unprecedented growth in technology. Partly due to the Cold War, a higher value was beginning to be placed on information than on industry. Industrial jobs left the more developed countries for countries that were still transitioning from the agricultural age to the industrial age. Communication devices began to be improved at a faster rate, and in 1981, IBM home personal computers hit the market. When the Internet became commercially available in 1995, the Information Age really kicked off. Today, Information Technology (IT) has become an industry unto itself.

In 1982, Congress enacted education legislation for the high school graduating class of 2000. Realizing the effects of globalization as early as 1982, Congress had the foresight to make some sweeping changes in our educational system in order to make students more prepared for the Information Age. Changes were instituted so that the High School graduating class of 2000 would have the full effect of a new educational system. This is where the term "millennials" comes from in describing the generation that graduated High School after 2000.

Because the fall of the Berlin Wall in 1989 occurred in the midst of the transition between industrial and information ages, it is attached as a significant date in describing the Information Age. The event that most signified our entering the Information Age was when the internet went public in 1995. Who actually invented the Internet, and when, is still hotly debated, but even former presidential hopefuls don't debate that it was commercialized in 1995. Today, information is changing so fast, it is hard to keep up with. The easiest way to realize this is to consider how fast cell phones change. Smart phones can do more now than PCs could do a few years ago, and almost everyone has one.

Information Age

- » 1981—IBM personal Computers hit the U.S. market
- » 1982—Congress enacts new education legislation aimed at graduating class of 2000
- » 1989—Berlin wall falls, signaling the end of the Cold War
- » 1995—The Internet goes public
- » 1995-present—Shift happens

To drive this point home, there are a series of presentations on YouTube called *Shift Happens*. The first Shift Happens presentation came out in 2007, and was designed to express the changes brought about by the globalization of our economy and the advent of the Information Age. Here are a few of the points it makes:

- » Predicted that the top 10 jobs of 2010 did not even exist in 2004
- » Average person today will have 10-14 different jobs by the time he or she is 38
- » 1 in 4 employees today has had his or her job for less than a year
- » 1 in 2 employees has had his or her job for less than 5 years
- » Technology information doubles every 2 years

So What!

So, what does this history lesson have to do with resistance? It is all about Newton's first law of motion (I know, you thought this was going to be easier than the history lesson).

Newton's First Law states that a *body remains at rest or in motion with a constant velocity unless acted upon by an external force.*

In other words, if something is at rest, it will stay at rest until some force moves it; or, something that is motion will stay in motion at the same speed until some force slows it down or speeds it up. If you are at rest, it takes a lot of energy to get you moving—much more energy than to keep you moving. Once moving, it takes more force for you to stop and change directions than to keep moving at the same speed and direction. That is exactly what the industrial age has done. Its effects are still in motion today, and those effects are a form of resistance to your gift. Let me explain.

The industrial age trained managers to make sure profits on the bottom line were good. Managers thought of workers as numbers to be controlled in order to perform a certain task. It was the task that was important, and if you did not perform the task well enough, or you did not like the task, you would be replaced by another person who would perform that task. Personality, talent, and gifts did not enter into management decisions. Your skill at performing a task is all that mattered. Since the worth of the task was a set amount of production costs, then your salary did not really depend on your gift, but on what the company decided the task was worth.

Almost all management theories still in practice today originated during the Industrial Age. Management of numbers is what is viewed as important, and lip service is given to valuing employees. Employees are valued just enough to be attracted to perform a certain task required by a company. Today's Industrial Age companies are filled by managers of the generation we call baby-boomers. If you work in a company and your boss is a baby-boomer, he more than likely manages with an Industrial Age mindset. That mindset values skills, not talent or gift. They work in an atmosphere of competition, which is based on fear. Competition gives the notion that one person has to be better at a task than another one, or he will be fired. To the Industrial Age, baby-boomer manager, people are just numbers that affect profits.

The millennial generation (those born in 1982 and later) grew up in the Information Age. That generation's way of thinking was formed in a school system that was radically different from the baby-boomers system, or even the system of Generation X (those born between 1964 and 1982). Millennials grew up with computers, cell phones, DVDs, and MP3 players. Their schooling encouraged them to work together on projects, and to develop innovation, ingenuity, and the ability to think. By contrast, former generations were trained to be rugged individualists and to be completely self-reliant. Millennials were encouraged to use creativity.

Information Age Millennials require leadership to guide them. Leadership seeks to bring out the greatest talent and ability in a person, and then place that person on a team where he will perform the best. Unfortunately, most of the gifted Millennials entering the work force do not find the leadership they need in order to thrive. Instead they find Industrial Age managers telling them what to do. These managers feel threatened or challenged by Millennials who constantly ask "Why?" To the manager, this is not an appropriate question, and the answer is often "Because I said so." To the Millennial, asking "Why?" means he just wants all the information (remember it is the Information Age) he can get, so that he does a good job the first time. The Millennial wants to use a multiplicity of resources to accomplish a task, and the more guidance and information he can get up front, the better a job he can do. This way of thinking is completely lost on most Industrial Age managers.

The consequence of the clash between Industrial Age managers and companies, and their Information Age workforce is twofold: first, there is a huge degree of dissatisfaction among millennial employees; second, there is a huge amount of innovation and creativity that is being stifled. My opinion is that our current economic upheaval is partly due to the clash of the two ages. The momentum of Industrial Age thought in management (managers still being trained by Industrial Age, baby-boomer experts) is causing resistance to fully moving into the Information Age. The U.S. cannot enter into a new age of prosperity if we continue to try to live in the Industrial Age. It is creativity and innovation that have been the hallmarks of our country's greatness. In the past, the creativity and innovation of Americans ushered in prosperity by capitalizing on the Industrial Revolution. To realize a new wave of prosperity, we have to again rely on our creativity and innovation, but this time in the areas of an Information Revolution.

Harris Poll

The disconnect between Information Age employees and Industrial Age managers has many organizations running around in circles, and not knowing why. According to Steven Covey's book, *The 8th Habit*[34], Harris Interactive (the originators of the Harris poll) polled 23,000 U.S. residents employed full time within key industries and in key functional areas. Here are some of the most stunning findings:

- » Only 37 percent said they have a clear understanding of what their organization is trying to achieve and why.
- » Only 1 in 5 was enthusiastic about his organization's goals
- » Only 1 in 5 workers said he had a clear line of sight between his tasks and his team's and organization's goals.
- » Only half were satisfied with the work they accomplished at the end of the week.

---

34   *The 8th Habit*, Stephen Covey

- » Only 15 percent felt that their organization fully enables them to execute key goals.
- » Only 15 percent felt they worked in a high trust environment.
- » Only 17 percent felt their organization fosters open communication that is respectful of differing opinions and that results in new and better ideas
- » Only 10 percent felt that their organization holds people accountable for results.
- » Only 20 percent fully trusted the organization they work for.
- » Only 13 percent have high trust, highly cooperative working relationships with other groups or departments.

To put it another way; if, say, a football team had these same scores:

- » Only 4 of 11 players on the field would know which goal was theirs.
- » Only 2 of the 11 would care.
- » Only 2 of the 11 would know what position they play and know exactly what they are supposed to do.
- » And all but 2 players would, in some way, be competing against their own team members rather than the opponent.

The Enemy

Recognizing where your resistance is coming from is half of the battle. In the *Art of War*[35], Sun Tzu said two of the things you MUST know in order to have victory, are:

1. You must know yourself
2. You must know the enemy

We have spent a good deal of time talking about the importance of knowing who you really are. Even if you have done the work to really know

---

35 *Art of War*, Sun Tzu

yourself, you can still be defeated. There are forces that do not want you to succeed. If you don't think so, I would say you are either naïve, or you have not been very successful yet.

The enemy can mean different things to different people. Some of my friends automatically think Satan is the enemy. I certainly believe Satan is real and that he is powerful, but he is not God. Only God is omniscient, omnipresent and omnipotent. For the Christian, Satan is already defeated, and I think we give him much too much credit.

I think our biggest enemy is *inertia*. Inertia is the same thing as Newton's first law of motion. The way I use it here, is that anybody, or thing, that is at rest, tends to stay at rest. It takes a force to get something or someone to move. That is Newton's second law of motion. It says that Force = Mass times Acceleration (F=ma). If you want to get something big to move fast, it is going to take a lot of force. I am sure you have heard this analogy before, but it takes much more power to move a jet airliner from a start to takeoff, than it does to keep it in the air at a constant speed. The same is true of a car. It takes a lot more gas to get the car from 0 to 60 miles per hour, than to keep it at 60 once you get there. The same is true for you. Once you know who you are and what your gift is, there is a huge enemy out there that wants to keep you at rest, right where you are. Satan can be a good part of that force, but the biggest enemy is inertia. You will need a big reason to want to exert the force necessary to overcome the enemy and claim the victory you were destined to achieve.

Finding the reason that is big enough for you to put out the force necessary to be victorious is the subject of *The Holy Hand Grenade*. Not finding it is what causes almost all defeats. Don't let that happen to you.

Conclusion

Have you discovered your gift? If not, did you take the *StrengthsFinder 2.0* test and find your top strength? Remember that your top strength in this test is what I call your gift.

How does your personality enable you to use your gift? If you are having trouble with this question ask your best friend, spouse, or mentor to work through it with you. As Napoleon Hill said, you have to Think to Grow Rich, so this question deserves some serious thought.

What are you doing to develop your gift? Once you have defined what it is, your gift should be so exciting to you that you would want to spend the rest of your life developing and giving your gift. This should be a labor of love, not a duty or a drudge.

Be aware that once you start moving in the direction of your quest you will probably get to face that horrible creature called resistance, or the Killer Rabbit in King Arthur's terms. To overcome resistance we usually will need more firepower for the fight than we can muster ourselves. This is where you may need help from someone on your team to join you in the fight. You will definitely need to have a big enough reason for persisting against resistance to get what you want, and that is the subject of the next question.

Part IV

The Third Question

Chapter 18

The Third Question

A STORY FROM ANCIENT TIMES TELLS about a young man who travelled a great distance to find the wisest man on earth, Socrates. He finally arrived in Athens, walked up to the muscular old philosopher and said, "O great Socrates, I come to you seeking wisdom."

Without speaking a word, Socrates led the young man through the streets of Athens, to the sea and into chest-deep water. Then he asked, "What do you want?"

"Wisdom, O wise Socrates," said the young man with great expectation.

Socrates put his strong hands on the man's shoulders and pushed him under the water. Thirty seconds later Socrates let him up. "What do you want?" he asked again.

"Wisdom," the young man sputtered, "O great and wise Socrates."

Socrates crunched him under again. Thirty seconds passed, thirty-five. Forty. Socrates let him up. The man was gasping. "What do you want, young man?"

Between heavy, heaving breaths, the fellow wheezed, "Wisdom, O wise and wonderful…"

Socrates jammed him under again. Forty seconds passed. Fifty. "What do you want?"

"Air!" the young man gasped. "I need air!"

"When you want wisdom as much as you have just wanted air, then you will have wisdom."

In this old story, the young man came to Socrates seeking wisdom. Socrates showed him that until he sought something with a great desire, he would not have it. Most people do not seek anything, and they wonder why they don't have anything. One of my favorite questions to ask people is, "If you could do anything for a career or income, what do you really want to do?" Only about five percent of all the people I have asked can answer that question, and of the five percent, only about half are either doing what they want to do, or have a plan to do it.

I would really like to ask people what they seek, but I am not sure most people would even understand the question. That is because the word *seek* is not used very often in today's vocabulary. The dictionary defines *seek* as;

Seek—To go in search of, or look for.

Seeking involves action and effort. You can't seek, and do nothing. That would merely be wishing, wanting, or hoping. When you seek something, it is like going on a quest. In the beginning of this book, one of the questions the bridge keeper asked King Arthur was "What is your quest?" And Arthur's reply was "I seek the Holy Grail." He knew what he was seeking, and like the young man seeking wisdom, he was willing to do whatever was required to find what he was seeking.

So, the third question is "What do you seek?"

I think most people would be inclined to skip the first two questions and go right to "What do you seek?" I probably would. But skipping the first two questions would be a big mistake. If you don't really know who you are and what your gift is, it is not possible that you will seek the right thing. That would be like the person going on the airplane ride to Washington, D.C., described in chapter 4. If you don't know where you are starting from, you won't be able to get where you want to go. So, if you skipped to this chapter without reading the previous chapters, it probably won't help you too much.

The Greek word for *seek* has the connotation that you don't just seek once but that seeking is a continuous process. Seeking means trying to acquire something, but the word *seek* is not used very much in today's vernacular. Let me ask you the third question a few different ways, and you can choose which one has the greatest impact on you.

- What do you seek?
- What do you desire?
- What do you really want?
- What do you really want to do?
- What do you really want to go after?
- What is your purpose?
- What is your mission?
- What have you been chosen for?
- What is your calling?
- What will give you a sense of accomplishment?
- What is going to fill the void in your life?
- What will bring you joy?
- What will really make you happy?
- What is your destiny?

This leads us to another misunderstood word, *desire*. In order to seek continuously after something, you have to desire it so strongly that you will let nothing get in your way. There is a proverb in the Bible about this topic. It is attributed to King Solomon, the wisest man in the world, according to the Bible. That proverb goes like this:

> *"Hope deferred makes the heart grow sick,*
> *But desire fulfilled is a tree of life.*[36]*"*

---

36 *The Holy Bible*, Proverbs 13:12

King Solomon was wise indeed. What was true 4000 years ago is still true today. The world is filled with people whose hearts are sick. They have hoped and hoped, but to no avail. If their desires could be fulfilled, they would come back to life and be able to give some of their life to others. So, why are so many people, and perhaps you, broken hearted? Why don't they know what they really want, or seek? The answer lies in two words: desire, and passion.

Desire

Napoleon Hill dedicated an entire chapter in his world famous book, *Think and Grow Rich*[37], to desire. At the beginning of the chapter he boldly states, "Desire is the starting point of all achievement." Without a burning desire, your chances of answering the third question are zero.

The dictionary defines Desire as:

That **internal act**, which, by influencing the will, makes us proceed to action.

So desire has a few characteristics.

1. Desire is internal
2. Desire influences your will
3. Desire causes action

Does everyone have desire? Yes, we all have a great desire for something. You were born with it; it is a gift, and your life's mission is to fulfill your desire. King David wrote:

> *"Delight yourself in the LORD; and He will give you the **desires** of your heart.*[38]*"*

I find it interesting that the Bible says your desire resides in your heart. To a western mind, that doesn't really make a lot of sense. We usually think of the heart as an organ that pumps blood, but it isn't referred to as

---

37 *Think and Grow Rich*, Napoleon Hill
38 *The Holy Bible*, Psalm 37:4

an organ in Scripture. The Greek definition makes this clearer for us. The Greek word for heart is *kardía*. Kardia (*heart*) is "the affective center of our being" and the capacity of moral preference (volitional desire, choice). The heart is the desire-producer that makes us tick, and it is our desire-decisions that establish who we really are.

Heart is mentioned over 800 times in Scripture, but never referring to the literal physical pump that drives the blood. That is, "heart" is only used as our "desire-producer" (both in the Old Testament and New Testament).

In Dr. Caroline Leaf's research on how the brain functions, she mentions that researchers have found some very interesting facts about the heart. There is scientifically proven evidence that a direct connection between the brain and the heart exists. The heart actually has a function as a sort of "second brain." Not that the heart actually forms thoughts like your brain does, but it is a center of emotions and feelings that become memories in the brain.

So, we all know each person has a heart. Since you have a heart, then you also have a desire that flows from your heart. Seeking the desire that flows from your heart is the quest of *The Holy Hand Grenade*. The desire of your heart is intensely personal and unique to you. You have the choice to fulfill that desire, or to ignore it. If God placed that desire in your heart from before you were born, and he wants you to fulfill it, then your greatest happiness and joy come from your desire.

Then why do so many people walk around without evidence of desiring anything? They don't seem to want anything bad enough to do anything about it. That question has plagued me for a long time. I have found several answers, one of which may be for you. If not knowing your desire is an issue for you, then reflecting on the reasons in the next chapter should give you an answer.

Chapter 19

Eleven Reasons Why People Do Not Know Their Burning Desires

1. **Desire is stopped by a hard heart.**

Why would anyone have a hard heart? Because he does do not know he is loved. Knowing you are loved enables your heart to receive from the one who loves you. This isn't mushy stuff for weak people. It is the stuff that strong and confident people have—stuff that people who lack confidence do not have. In most cases, a hard heart is the result of someone letting you down. You were counting on them, and they did not come through for you, so your trust in the one you loved is shaken. This could be the result of a divorce, a bad romance, the death of someone you loved, abandonment by someone who should have loved you, or many other reasons. Often, people who have had these experiences end up blaming God. They will often say things such as, "If God is so good, how could he let this (or make this) happen to me." The seed of doubt that your Father loves you has been sown, and a hard heart begins to develop.

2. **You don't know what you can do.**

If you think you cannot do something, you may not even try.

"The will to do springs from the knowledge that we *can* do." [39]

Maybe your parents, a friend, or a teacher told you what you could and could not do as a child. Since they loved you, you assumed they were right. If you have the fear of failure, as most of us do to some degree, then why would you try to pursue the desire of your heart if you **assume** you can't have it? This is a place where assuming things, without knowing them to be facts, can be very detrimental to a happy life. Having someone in your life to challenge you to try things you think you cannot do could really open your eyes to more possibilities.

Drill Sergeants did some of this for me, but you may want to find a less invasive means.

3. **Desire is a bad word.**

I remember from Sunday school lessons that *desire* seemed to be evil. I perceived that if I had desires, they were considered to be evil desires; as if *evil* and *desire* always went together. That thought comes largely from misuse of the word *desire*. If you use the word *desire* to mean uncontrolled lust, then yes, it probably is evil. But that is not what desire always means. Some people, usually overzealous religious people, also say you should just be happy with what you have, and you should not desire anything else. That is why I agree with the Hospitaller from the *Kingdom of Heaven* movie. I put no stock in *religion*, as that is man's invention. I do, however, agree with what God says, and he says, "Desire fulfilled is a tree of life." In fact, it is God who gave you a (good) desire and put it in your heart—and he wants you to fulfill it. So, if God gave you a desire in the first place, and "Faithful is He who calls you, and He also will bring it to pass[40]", then God wants you to have the desire he planted in your heart from before you were born. That desire is a gift from him to you and is an ultimate source of joy in this life.

---

39 *As A Man Thinketh*, James Allen

40 *The Holy Bible*, 1 Thessalonians 5:24

4. **You don't know who you are.**

If you don't know who you are, then, by default, you are who someone else says you are. If this is your case, you will be trying to fulfill someone else's desire, and not your own. You will have a false sense of what success means, thinking the person you allowed to determine your future actually knows you as well as your Father does. This reason particularly strikes home with me. I allowed someone else to tell me what success was, rather than defining it for myself. I tried to be a dominant leader-type personality, because I admired people with those kinds of personalities. When I finally realized who I really was, I stopped trying to be a success for someone else and started doing things the way my Father created me to do them. Trust me on this one: the second way works much better. Once you start acting as the person you really are, it becomes much easier to get in touch with the desire of your heart. Then, you begin to realize that your desire is exactly right for you. Do not allow anyone to tell you what you should desire. Shakespeare said, "To Thine own self be true.[41]"

5. **You don't know your gift.**

If you don't know your gift, you don't know how you are supposed to fit in. If you don't know these two things, you won't value what you can contribute to the world, and you won't feel like you are making a difference. When I ask people what they really want to do, even the ones who have no idea, know this much: they know they want to make a difference somehow. Making a difference comes from knowing your gift, developing it to the point where you are a professional, and then giving it freely (as opposed to "for free"). The price of knowing your gift is this: "From everyone who has been given much, much will be required; and to whom they entrusted much, of him they will ask all the more.[42]" This means that once you know your gift, you have to be prepared to give it. Using your gift and giving it will bring you a great deal of satisfaction. It has everything to do with the desire of your heart.

---

41 *Hamlet*, Act 1, Scene 3, William Shakespeare

42 *The Holy Bible*, Luke 12:48

6. **You don't know your Father.**

Your "identity," that sense of being approved for who you are, comes from your Father. Knowing and completely understanding that you are approved of, and loved, is what gives you confidence and boldness. Having a desire that burns within you requires a certain amount of confidence. It is the kind of confidence that knows "Even though you walk through the valley of the shadow of death, you will fear no evil, because He is with you.[43]" You know you cannot fail when it comes to your burning desire, because it comes from your Father, and if "God is for you, then who is against you?[44]"

7. **There is something wrong about the desire to be rich.**

I have to admit that I struggled with this idea at one time, and I didn't know why. So I wanted to find out where this idea came from. I found that it came from two sources: religion and politics.

Religion.

The Bible specifically says, "It is the blessing of the Lord that makes rich, and He adds no sorrow to it.[45]" The Bible also lays out the blessings of wealth and the curses of lack.[46] On the other hand, we are not to worship money as our "source." The Bible is very clear that only God is our source, and He wants to bless us with abundance[47]. A misinterpretation of the Sermon on the Mount (also known as the Beatitudes) has caused some of the confusion. In the first part of that sermon, Jesus says, "Blessed are the poor in spirit, for theirs is the Kingdom of heaven.[48]" "Poor in spirit" means those who are not spiritually arrogant; it does not mean "poor in money."

The take-from-the-rich and redistribute-the-wealth idea comes from

---

43 *The Holy Bible*, Psalm 23:4

44 *The Holy Bible*, Romans, 8:31

45 *The Holy Bible*, Proverbs 10:22

46 *The Holy Bible*, Deuteronomy 28

47 *The Holy Bible*, 3 John1:2, James 4:2-3, Ephesians 3:20, Matthew 7:7-11

48 *The Holy Bible*, Matthew 5:3

the European tradition of monarchies, where only the aristocracy and monarchs were wealthy. All western Christian religions (denominations) grew up in Europe under these conditions, and that has caused a lot of harm.

The early Christian Church (before it devolved into denominations of religion) gave from what it had out of love, not obligation. Early Christians were not told to give, or compelled to give. They had an understanding of sowing and reaping, not stealing and redistributing. As the Christian Church grew in size its organizational structure took on the form of the only governments that existed at the time—monarchies. The Christian monarchy-style organization, with all the same attitudes as secular monarchies, still pervades today in many "Christian" religions.

Politics

Politicians know there are more people that are broke (financially struggling) than there are people that are rich. That means more voters are broke than are rich. Rather than helping them gain more wealth, politicians tend to offer broke people some form of security. The security they offer will come from them (the Government), if you vote for them. They want your vote so they can stay in power. Politicians have become the new aristocracy, and many people feel helpless to do anything about it. People seeking security from the government seem to have forgotten that the "Government" is of, for, and by the people. The Government can't give people security without taking the means of that security from the people. It is an illusion that some politicians are masters at creating.

If politicians can keep you broke, and you feel okay about it, they can keep their power. Since there are fewer rich people than broke people, and politicians can't control the rich people, then they try to make rich people look like bad guys. It becomes an "evil" thing to be like one of the rich, since the rest of us are good people, and we're all broke (so the politicians' thinking goes).

8. **You feel guilty about being successful.**

This is closely related to number 7 (thinking there is something wrong with being rich), but it is slightly different. Being successful can mean different things to different people. One can have success in marriage, relationships, sports, or a career. In order to keep things simple, I will only use success in making money in this example, but the concept applies to all definitions.

If you feel guilty about being successful, chances are that one of these is the reason:

a. You hurt someone on the way to becoming successful. If you cheated, lied, or stole to become successful, you probably should feel guilty, and you should make the situation right.

b. You think you possess some special quality that others don't possess. Because you believe you are exceptionally beautiful, talented, intelligent, or charming, you feel guilty that you have achieved what others cannot.

c. You think you benefited from breaks or opportunities others cannot get. Basically, you think your success was purely luck, so you don't think you deserve it.

d. You think you did it all by yourself. Your self-determination and will power are superior to that of others. You think your success was the sole result of your hard work, your effort.

I have news for you. It is not all about you. Anything you possess that allowed you to become successful was a gift to you from your Father. You may have worked hard to develop your gifts and become successful, but everyone has a gift that can be developed to be just as successful, or more so. Your success is meant to inspire others to become all they were created to be.

God warns us about thinking we are responsible for our own success. In the book of Deuteronomy, chapters 7 and 8, God tells about all the promises and gracious (unmerited and undeserved favor) dealings he has for his people. In Chapter 8, verse 17[49], God says,

"You may say in your heart, 'My power and the strength of my hand

---

49   *The Holy Bible*, Deuteronomy 8:17-18

made me this wealth', but you shall remember the Lord your God, for it is He who gives you power to make wealth, that He may confirm His covenant which He swore to your fathers, as it is this day."

If you are successful and you feel guilty about it, the reason is that you are not giving the credit where it is due. God gave you the power to become successful by giving you your personality, your gift, your good looks, your charm, and the desire to do something great with it. But you were not singled-out as an exception for success by God. He also gave gifts to others, as well. Your giving the Father the credit for your success allows others to see how much the Father also loves them, and has blessed them.

If you feel guilty about being successful, it is a good indicator to you. Your guilt is misplaced. You should not feel guilty that you are successful and others are not. If you feel guilty, let it help you realize that you should use your success to help others find their own successes. There is plenty of success to go around for everyone. Overcoming this guilt may well be the key to unlocking the desire of your heart.

9. **You think you have to do it alone.**

Any burning desire you have will, of necessity, require other people to make it come about. The English poet John Donne said, "No man is an island.[50]" When we think we have to do it all by ourselves, our desire looks to be unachievable. But when we realize that God "is able to do far more abundantly beyond all that we ask or think, according to the power that works within us[51]", then we realize we can have whatever our hearts desire. Your desire will be linked to someone else's desire, so your working together will make you both happy. For example, if you want to write a book, you may think it is all up to you. But, after you get started, you will realize someone will need to edit it; someone will have to print it and publish it; someone will have to market it; and someone will have to buy and read it. The same will be true for whatever you desire; it will involve other people.

---

50 *Devotions upon emergent occasions and several steps in my sickness - Meditation XVII*, 1624, John Donne

51 *The Holy Bible*, Ephesians 3:20

10. You don't know what motivates you financially

Financially speaking, people are motivated in one of three ways:

- » security
- » comfort or
- » wealth

No one of these is better or worse than the other, but being confused about how you are financially motivated can lead to confusion about what you desire. When I ask people which of these financial motives is their hot button, most people will say "wealth." The problem is that their actions and thinking don't support what they say. Someone who is truly wealth-motivated has developed the habits of delayed gratification and saving, and they are willing to take calculated risks. They also have spent time, energy, and money to get the education they will need to create and keep their wealth. When people are really honest with themselves, they may like the idea of someday being wealthy, but they are really motivated by comfort or security. An indicator that one is comfort-motivated is that they will work overtime or get a masters degree in order to get a nicer house, a better car, or take a great vacation every year. Most men, and almost all women, are really motivated by security. The thought of not being able to pay their bills, or losing their home is what gets them out of bed to go to work every day. It may also be what keeps them from looking beyond their job for the desire of their heart.

Knowing how you are financially motivated will allow you to figure out if what you want to do will actually achieve the desired end. If you are motivated by security, then figuring out how much money it will take for you to be financially secure will allow you to move on to doing something great with your life. If comfort is your thing, then a career that provides the comforts you seek will allow you to focus on other people in addition to the nice things of life. If wealth is your desire, then having a plan for it, which incorporates enough security for your spouse, will make life a lot easier.

11. **Some P.E.S.T. got in your way that you cannot overcome on your own**

You may have started down the path of trying to find out what you really wanted in life, only to be stopped by some kind of PEST. Did you have a Holy Hand Grenade that you could lob at the PEST to blow it up? Did you ask for help to overcome your weakness?

In the scene from *Monty Python and the Holy Grail*, the PEST was a furry rodent called the Killer Rabbit. For my purposes, I will use PEST as an acronym for someone or something that wants to stop you on your quest to get what you seek.

P—people. Do the people you associate with really want to help you succeed, or do they want to hold you back? Sometimes the people we love the most, or who have been our best friends, don't really want us to make it. They have grown comfortable with where they are, and if you move on without them, they may feel threatened. To follow your quest and get you what you seek, you may have to change some of the people you associate with.

E—emotions. Most people are more emotional than they realize. Almost all sales and marketing efforts are aimed at our emotions. Without even knowing it, most of our decisions are made entirely based on emotions, or are heavily influenced by them. To get what you seek, you need to listen to the reasoning side of your thinking and ask for wisdom, rather than submitting to your emotions. Your emotions will almost always have you quit somewhere on your quest. They are probably the biggest PEST. Dr. Don Colbert wrote a book called *Deadly Emotions*[52], in which he describes emotions that will not only stop you from getting what you seek, but may actually kill you. Emotions like guilt, fear, shame, worry, unforgiveness, and anger are certainly deadly.

S—survival. Our most basic instinct is for survival. Unfortunately, this instinct traps many into only seeking survival. In today's world, this translates into only being concerned about paying the bills. If all of your actions are geared to just surviving to the weekend, you have been trapped

---

52 *Deadly Emotions*, Dr Don Colbert

by the PEST of survival. This is a sure way to be stopped on your quest. When you seek abundance instead of just survival, it (abundance) has a way of manifesting.

T—thinking. "For as he thinks within himself, so is he.[53]" This proverb is literally true. The P, E and S of PEST all have to do with how and what you think. Your thinking could be a PEST that needs to change, or it could be the greatest asset on your quest. The great thing about your thinking is that it is under your control. You get to choose how you think.

Asking for help is your Holy Hand Grenade when you run into a PEST. I find that many people are either too frozen in fear to ask for help, or they don't know to whom they can go.

Ultimately, the best person you can go to when you face an obstacle of fear is your Father. Whatever you fear, fears God. If He is for you, who can be against you, and in all these things you overwhelmingly conquer through Him who loves you.[54] These fears can manifest as the thought that:

- » Time is running out—it is too late for you
- » You aren't good enough—low self-esteem, not trusting in who you are, or your gift
- » What if you fail—too much concern about what others may think
- » What if you succeed—too much concern about what others may think
- » You don't know where to start

Each of these fears can be very real and debilitating. The question you need to ask yourself is this: are you going to let them stop you, or are you going to blow them up and keep moving?

---

53 *The Holy Bible*, Proverbs 23:7
54 *The Holy Bible*, Romans 8:31, 37

Chapter 20

Passion

As with some of the other words I have been using to answer what you seek, the word *passion* is also often misconstrued. This time however, I will start by telling you what *passion* is not.

People who do not know how to describe or define passion will often use other words to describe it. You will hear words such as *enthusiasm* and *motivation* used as synonyms for passion. However, these words do not hit the mark. I have found there are very few people who are genuinely passionate about what they do. Passionate people have a very difficult time understanding those who are not as passionate about their purpose as they are, and the passionate cannot tell you how to acquire passion. Passionate people will try to help impassionate people by getting them to be enthusiastic or by motivating them. While passionate people usually are very motivated, and they exhibit a lot of enthusiasm, it is not necessarily true that someone who displays enthusiasm or seems motivated is actually passionate about what he is doing. It is as if enthusiasm and motivation are the natural byproducts of passion.

Enthusiasm can come and go, while *passion* lasts. Enthusiasm is a feeling or emotion that can be manufactured at will, and it can result in action, but that action is usually short lived. Because enthusiasm can be created, it can also be manipulated, either by yourself, or by someone who is charismatic enough to cause you to be enthusiastic. If enthusiasm is created but does not spring from passion, it will not get you the desire of your heart. Other people will also be able to tell that your enthusiasm is not real, and that it does not come from passion.

In the movie *Master and Commander*[55], Russell Crowe plays an English captain of a Man-of-War ship during the Napoleonic Wars. A scene in the movie shows officers of the ship having dinner in the wardroom. Crowe's character, Captain Aubrey, was asked if he would tell an anecdote about Lord Admiral Nelson, a hero of the English Navy. Captain Aubrey said he had spoken with Nelson twice: "The second time he told me a story about how someone offered him a boat cloak on a cold night. He said, no, he didn't need it. He was quite warm. His zeal for king and country kept him warm." As Aubrey looked around the dining table, he noticed the look of disbelief on the face of his friend, the ship's doctor. He continued, "I know it sounds absurd, and were it from another man, you would cry out, 'oh, what pitiful stuff' and dismiss it as **mere enthusiasm**...but with Nelson, you felt your heart glow."

In this scene, Captain Aubrey makes the point that there is a difference between mere enthusiasm and genuine passion. The difference is huge. The heart-glowing passion to do something great with our lives is what we all hope for. This is the kind of passion that drives one forward in the face of overwhelming odds. This is the kind of passion that seems obsessive to others. It does not know the word defeat. It is the kind of passion that allows one to go the extra mile, or even the extra ten miles, and do it with confidence and vigor. It is this kind of passion to a purpose that is the key to all great success. People with this kind of passion exude confidence. They have a contagious optimism that stirs men's hearts. This is what Captain Aubrey felt as he stood next to Admiral Nelson on that cold night. It is the kind of passion we go to movies to see, and dream about.

Motivation is what we need in order to keep moving. Business leaders and sales managers will often go to great expense to orchestrate

---

55 *Master and Commander: The Far Side of the World*, 2003, Twentieth Century Fox Film Corporation

motivational events for their teams. They bring in motivational speakers to present emotional talks designed to "pump up" their staffs. They try to motivate them in order to get them back out on the trail, and to help them "keep on keeping on." These motivational events are designed to make sure they hit the next goal.

Please do not hear what I am not saying. I am not saying that motivation, enthusiasm, or goals are bad things. What I am saying is that having enthusiasm, being motivated, or reaching for goals without desire and passion will only give you very temporary results. If you are passionate about your desire, you will need no one to pump you up. If you are truly passionate about what you are doing, you will naturally be enthusiastic, and everyone around you will know it. If someone has to set goals for you, and then manage you to make sure you hit them, it is a sure sign you are not passionate about what you are doing. All the books and management theories about goal setting were written to make people do things they do not have a desire or passion for. Also, those books and management theories were written by people who have high D-style personalities. High D personalities can make themselves do things they don't want to do by giving themselves swift (mental) kicks in their rear ends. If you are not a high D personality, and you could hear the self talk of one of these Dominant, Directing, Doers, it would probably scare you half to death. Even the D personalities can't force themselves to hit goals forever. They burn out too. They only *appear* to be successful without knowing their desires, but somewhere in their lives, there are huge holes in their hearts.

The challenge is that we have very few examples to follow of people who really have passion. Even when you find such a person, he or she never seems to be able to explain to the rest of us how to get such a wonderful thing. People who are pursuing their desires with passion cannot conceive of a world without passion. They do not understand others who don't possess the passions they have. Two of the most successful men I know in the business world are both men of purpose and passion. As I tried to discuss this subject of how to acquire the passion they both have, I could see puzzled looks of disbelief on their faces. It was as if I was speaking Martian to them.

What Passion Is

If desire comes from inside you and is what creates action, then Passion is the power behind that action.

Desire → Action

Passion → Power

The ancient Greek word for passion is *paskho*. It means "to suffer; having intense feeling."

Suffering and *passion* did not seem to go together, to me, so I had to look up the word *suffer*. I thought it meant intense pain, like from torture or a disease, but what it really means is to submit to, or to be forced to endure something. It also means to put up with something that is inevitable or unavoidable. So, in other words, being passionate means **to be compelled by intense emotion, being able to endure and put up with the unavoidable.**

Today, when we say someone is passionate, we usually use it in a sexual context. That is **not** how I am using it here; but if you can understand the intensity of being passionate in a sexual way, then the same intensity can be applied to the desire of your heart. When we say someone is passionate about something, we mean he has an intense desire for something that radiates from him, and that it does not dissipate. He is able to put up with things in his pursuit that someone without passion would not put up with. Passion, that intense compelling emotion, is the power that sets your desire in motion and keeps it moving. It is passion that creates momentum in accomplishing your desire and overcoming obstacles.

Without Desire and Passion

When we try to succeed without desire and passion in our endeavor, our only option becomes trying to fail our way to success. Many of the success books talk about how important failure is in becoming successful. In order to fail your way to success you need:

1. Discipline

2. Enthusiasm
3. Motivation
4. Goals
5. To be a Super Hero

Once you understand who you are, what your gift is, and what you desire, then you realize the following:

» Self Discipline is too much effort to do ***forever***
» Enthusiasm always fades
» Motivation stops when the motivator is gone
» Goals are a poor substitute for PASSION
» Most of us ain't Super Heroes

Discipline (even self discipline), enthusiasm, motivation, and goals are exerted from the outside. Either you, or someone else, **makes** you do something. On the other hand, desire and passion come from within. They are already there, trying to come out!

If you are told you will have to do something that will require discipline, and you must hit certain goals, doesn't it sound like it is going to be hard? If you are told you will need to go to training seminars in order to keep motivated, doesn't that tell you that what you will be doing won't be much fun? Yet, this is what a lot of us expect when it comes to doing something with our lives. We expect it to be hard, no fun, not exciting, and probably not too fulfilling. Without passion, the only way we can endure is by force.

On the other hand, if you are going to do something you desire and are passionate about, doesn't that sound like it would be exciting? If you put in long hours in pursuit of your desire, but it is something that gives you a lot of satisfaction, doesn't that beat watching the clock so you can go home? What if you woke up every day with the attitude that you can't wait to get back to doing the thing you love, with people who energize you? When this is your way of life, you may still have goals, but they are now a way of measuring where you are in respect to where you want to be.

Goals become a measure of tracking your own progress instead of being instruments of fear, driving you to keep your job.

What are you passionate about?

A good deal of why I decided to write this book was because I honestly felt that when God created me, he left out the passion chip. I could not find anything I wanted to put one hundred percent of myself into. I desperately wanted to find "it," even though I had no idea of what "it" was.

The more people I talked to about this subject, the more I found I was not alone. In fact, it was rare if I found someone who knew his desire and was passionate about it. Passionate people who are seeking to fulfill their heart's desire have the uncanny ability to persevere through hardships and persecution that would easily make someone who was merely enthusiastic stop dead in his tracks. I have always greatly admired people like that.

Part of why I did not feel passionate about anything was because I had a false idea of who I was. Another reason I didn't feel passionate was that I had no idea what my gift was, or that I even had a gift. This caused me to doubt my self-worth. Once I got those issues behind me, and started to understand more of the real me, I still wasn't passionate about anything in particular. I sort of expected that God would zap me with a lightning bolt one night, and the next morning I would be on fire for some worthy cause. Well, that didn't happen.

The only place I have ever read anything that talks about having or getting passion was in an obscure section in one of Robert Kiyosaki's books, *Before You Quit Your Job*. I have alluded to it once before, but in that book's section about spiritual money, Kiyosaki writes that his Rich Dad told him spiritual money was about doing a job not because you want to do it, but because it must be done. You know that way deep down inside yourself you are the one who is supposed to do it. He goes on to say that it could be

» Something that disturbs you because no one else is doing it
» Something that makes you angry or agitated
» Something that breaks your heart

> » Something that seems like an injustice or crime to you
> » Something that disturbs your sense of decency

My expectation was that doing something I was passionate about would be some heartfelt, humanitarian, churchy, kind of thing. Since I'm not really wired that way, it would have to take a rather large change in my life (like a lightning bolt) to make me feel that kind of passion about something. I really wondered what was wrong with me.

If you take a look at the list of things Kiyosaki's Rich Dad said involved spiritual money, they all have something in common. Each item on the list (and you can add many more items to the list) involves intense emotion. While I did not wake up feeling emotional about some great cause every day, I usually did wake up feeling agitated about something.

When I really thought about what it was that agitated me the most, and didn't stop meditating on it until I got to the root of it, I found my passion. So, I will share it with you, and for a good reason. It intensely bothers me when I see people, especially young people, who are completely wasting their lives. Whenever I saw a teenager all dressed in black, with more hardware piercing their bodies than Home Depot sells, and with more tattoos than a drunken sailor (no offense to sailors; remember I am married to one), I would be infuriated. I made myself go and talk to some of those kids, and I was astonished. Most of them were the nicest people you would ever meet, but they were completely lost. So then, I wanted to find their parents—and smack them.

I have gotten over my anger at those kids and their parents, but only because it led me to the root of the issue. Just drifting through life, and wasting it, is the worst insult you can give to the Father who gave you such wonderful gifts. I realized that was my issue too. When I finally figured that out, and could share it with my wife, her reaction was, "That's nice honey." I had a major breakthrough and that was the best she could respond? Here's the point. I found my passion, not hers. The thing that really upsets you may have no emotional effect on other people. That is because you are the one who is supposed to do something about it. They will have different missions to accomplish. So, don't worry about what anyone else thinks about your desire and passion. It only matters that you have one.

So, back to the question: what are you passionate about?

Are you a compassionate person who really does want to save the world, somehow? If so, which cause stirs your blood the most? Why? What is the root cause of your concern in this issue? Does what you want to do about it line up with your personality and gift? Will it be something you can devote the rest of your life to?

Are you passionate about businesses? If so, what exactly is it about business that really stirs your blood? When you are successful, how much money do you want to make, and what will you do with it? Why do you want to use your success in this way? Is building a business and becoming an expert something you want to do for the rest of your life? Are you willing to continue to work on your knowledge of your industry and never stop learning?

Are you really irritated, or even angry, about something? Is it something that has always angered you, or is it a onetime occurrence? If it has always angered you—why? Is there anyone else that is doing something about it? If not, what can you do about it? Is it a big enough issue that you are willing to put your whole self into fixing?

Is there a certain profession or activity that just thrills you every time you do it? You love the thought of being involved in that profession or activity, and you constantly think about it. Do your personality, your gift, and your way of thinking line up with this profession or activity? Can you see yourself becoming an expert in it?

Is there a group of people that moves your heart with passion or compassion? What is it about that group that moves you so much? What do you think you can contribute? Why you? What special gift do you have that the people in that group desperately need? Are you willing to dedicate yourself to those people for the rest of your life?

Passion feeds causes, builds businesses, rights injustices, creates beauty, and is the source of compassion. Without passion, people just go through the motions and try to survive. Without passion, a normal response to a challenge is, "Whatever." I absolutely hate that reply. It is dead, unemotional, uncaring, without thought, and apathetic. In my Marine Corps days, I would have said this was a DILLIGAS (Do I Look Like I Give A S_ _ _) attitude. That is a pathetic way to go through life, and nobody really wants it. People really do want to find something they are passionate about and can devote their lives to.

If all this describes what you are after, then there is an answer for you. But if you want the answer, you have to do three things: ask, seek and knock.

Chapter 21

Ask, Seek, Knock

THE ANSWERS TO YOUR GREATEST questions and issues come right out of heaven, literally. If you don't possess the desire of your heart, or you still don't know what it is, it is because you have not asked, sought, and knocked. You have to do all three. Jesus said that if you ask, it will be given to you. If you seek, you will find. If you knock, it will be opened for you.[56]

Asking

If you don't ask for something you are not going to get it. If you just expect people, or God, to read your mind and give you what you want, I have bad news for you: it doesn't work that way. You have to open your mouth and ask for what you want, and keep asking until you get it. If you want a good example of this, just watch any 4-year-old asking his mommy for something. Does he stop after the first no? Of course not, and neither did you when you were a kid. Children know how to wear their parents down, until they just give up and relent to their children's requests.

---

56   *The Holy Bible*, Matthew 7:7-11, Luke 11:9-13

There are a couple of conditions on your asking questions. First, whom you ask the question of is very important. That person has to be able to give you what you want. If it is not in his power to give you what you want, you are just wasting your time. If that 4-year-old wants an ice cream cone from his mommy, but mommy doesn't have the money for it, then the youngster will not get ice cream.

Second, when it comes to getting the desire of your heart, you cannot doubt you will receive after you have asked for it. Assuming the one you asked has the power to give you what you asked for, your job is to fully expect to receive it. If there is anything blocking your ability to receive your desire, find out what it is and meet that requirement. Then, ask again and expect to get what you asked for. If you don't expect to get what you asked for, I question whether you really wanted it in the first place. Why wouldn't you receive it? Do you feel unworthy? Do you feel you didn't earn it? Are these your issues, or does the one you are receiving from put them on you? Remember not to assume. You could be blocking your own answer without even knowing it.

Third, are you asking for the right thing? When you are asking for the desire of your heart, don't expect to get something that could actually harm you in the long run, especially if you are asking your Father. In the book of James, James says, "You ask and do not receive, because you ask with the wrong motives, so that you may spend it on your own pleasures.[57]" My first thought when I read this was, "Well, of course, I want to spend it on my own pleasures. What's this guy's problem?" There is a danger in asking for something that will just give you pleasure. Pleasure never lasts, and only creates the need for more pleasure. Pleasure will never make you happy. Whatever you ask for must be with the motive to find your desire and fulfill your purpose. It must involve using your gift and being the real you. Otherwise, what you ask for could actually hurt you.

Seeking

"Seeking" is the subject of *The Holy Hand Grenade*. Unfortunately, almost nobody seeks anything these days. Jesus was very direct in his

---

57 *The Holy Bible*, James 4:2-3

answer about seeking. He said, "Seek and you will find." The Greek use of the word *seek* implies a continuous state of seeking. So, it means "to keep seeking." Jesus' statement also says you "WILL find." It doesn't say you might find, or some will find and others won't. When you start to seek, you will need to do it with passion. You will have to endure and not give up until you find what you want. It is the idea of going on a quest. You have to seek with the mindset that you will not quit until you find what you are looking for. His promise to you is when you seek, you will find. When you really know your Father, you will hold him to his promises. He expects this from his kids, otherwise he wouldn't have made the promise in the first place.

Knocking

I could understand the idea of asking and seeking, but knocking didn't really make much sense to me; until recently. The image I have of knocking is of someone banging their knuckles on a big wooden door in the middle of the night. The doors of houses in ancient times were locked at night by placing a beam across the inside of the door. So, you had to knock at the door because it had to be opened from the inside. The beam on the inside of the door was meant to keep people out and protect those on the inside. If you knocked on someone's door at night, he would have to open the door from the inside to invite you in. You could not do it by yourself. So, if you are asking for something, and seeking for something, the requirement to knock means someone has to open the door for you and invite you inside. Knocking on the door and asking someone for something requires a degree of humility. You have to humble yourself to the degree that you recognize you don't have all the answers, you cannot find what you are looking for by yourself, and you can't open a locked door by yourself.

Chapter 22

Free Will

Your *free will* is an important factor in seeking your desire and fulfilling your quest. Some people have the idea there is no use in seeking anything because if they have a destiny, it will just happen. I don't believe that.

While in the Marine Corps, I was sent to Aviation Safety Officers (ASO) School. The main purpose of that school was to teach Aviation Safety Officers (each squadron had an officer who was appointed to this position) how to investigate aviation mishaps (crashes) in order to determine their causes. In some of the scenarios they gave us, there were no apparent causes. Sometimes, an incident appeared to be a freak of nature or that sometimes "_ _it happens." The biggest thing we were taught in ASO school was that "_ _it" doesn't just happen. There is always a reason.

The same thing is true with destiny. I believe God has a plan for your life and a destination in mind for you. His destination, the purpose for which you are destined, is far greater than anything you could come up with on your own. He gave you all the gifts you need to reach your destination and to be the greatest you. But He won't make you follow it. Ultimately, you have a choice. That choice is your free will.

If you look up the term *free will* on the Internet, standby to be confused. It seems no one agrees on what it is. Some people call it fate, or karma. Then, there are arguments about free will, destiny, and predestination. Even in Christianity, many denominations have different views on the subject. In fact, you will not find the term free will in the Bible. You will, however, find that God allows you to make choices. It is the ability to make choices about your future that I call *free will*.

There is a movie about free will called *The Adjustment Bureau*[58], in which Matt Damon plays a New York politician running for the US Senate. The entire movie is about how much choice we have in determining our own futures. In the movie, Matt Damon's character deviates from the predetermined plan set for him by the "Chairman." His stubborn resolve to make his own choices makes for a great movie with a powerful ending.

The Adjustment Bureau really caused me to think about this subject. Until I watched it, I just assumed my definition of free will was right. That was when I discovered there was no reference to the term *free will* in the Bible. After realizing my concept of free will was an assumption I had not questioned, I knew it was an important subject. I was taught—thinking back to my earliest recollection of religious education—that we were all created with free will. I took that for granted and never questioned it. I found there are numerous places where the Bible says we have "a choice." We have the choice whether to accept or refuse every gift we have from God. In addition to the fact that you don't have to earn a gift, you also don't have to receive a gift, or use it. You have that choice.

You have the ability to make your own choices in life. You can choose to operate in your real personality, or try to imitate someone else's. You have the choice to find your gift and use it, or to ignore it. You can choose to believe you are special and unique, or that you are just a "nobody". Henry Ford said, "Whether you think you can, or you think you can't, you are right." You choose what you believe.

You can also choose not to choose. In this case, you automatically enable someone else to choose for you. If you make the choice not to choose, then you allow someone else to manipulate you. A story about my mother helps to explain this. My mother was born in Berlin, Germany,

---

58 *The Adjustment Bureau*, 2011, Universal Pictures

and what later became known as East Berlin. After WWII she lived under communist rule, having just survived Nazi rule. Mom was a very gifted ice skater, and her personality was not well disposed to being controlled by her communist instructors. So, as a young woman, she decided to escape East Germany and continue her skating career in West Germany. Years later, after marrying and moving to America, she had the opportunity to visit with an old East Berlin skating friend; a prominent East German skating coach who had coached three world champion figure skaters. The coach was on an exhibition tour of the U.S. with her skaters (this was pre-1986 and East Germany was still Communist). Mom asked her friend why they didn't defect (besides not being well disposed to taking orders, Mom could also be very direct). Even though KGB agents followed them everywhere they went, they had plenty of opportunities to leave communism. My mother told me that her friend was so used to living under dictators (first with the Nazis and then the Communists) that she was not used to making any decisions on her own. The thought of having to deal with choices actually frightened her. It was easier to let someone else tell her what to do.

That story shocked me—at first. How could someone get so used to having someone else tell them what to do that they would voluntarily give up their free will? The more I thought about it, the more I saw the same thing happening in America. It takes less effort to allow someone else to make your choices than for you to choose. It also gives you someone else to blame. If you don't have what you want, after all, it wasn't your choice, and you had nothing to do with it. That is the classic definition of apathy. Many Americans are so apathetic, today, that they would rather have someone else make their decisions for them. Apathy leads to losing your liberty. When you give up your right to make choices, you are, in effect, trading your freedom for something else. Usually the thing most people will trade their freedom for is security. The unsuspecting, apathetic person will give away his freedom to someone who promises him some form of security in exchange.

Unknowingly, many people in "freedom loving countries" have surrendered their ability to choose to someone else. It is not that these people are stupid or lazy, as I used to think, but there is no way that an apathetic person will seek anything. There is no way that an apathetic person will seek anything.

So, I asked myself, "Why do people have such apathy?" The resounding answer I received was this: "They have no idea of how awesome they really are, and of the potential they are throwing away." Whenever I see people who do not want to make their own decisions, I know a few things about them. They don't know who they are. They have no idea they have special gifts, and consequently, they don't think they are of much value. They are probably just trying to survive, and they aren't seeking anything.

Only in a free society that guarantees life, liberty, and the pursuit of happiness can people choose to become all they were created for. Remember that passion is power, and when you don't have passion, you are actually giving your power to someone else to use. There are people (in business, politics and religion) who want to manipulate an apathetic population. What those people seek is power, and they seek it at someone else's expense. The freedom that the American Declaration of Independence guarantees for its citizens assumes that those citizens are not apathetic, and that they want to make choices for their lives. I think the best way to maintain that freedom is through each person seeking the desires of his heart and reaching for his full potential. If only five percent of Americans were operating in their gifts and seeking greatness, we would be living in a different world. There certainly wouldn't be any economic issues.

Chapter 23

More than Enough

Hopefully by now, you have a better idea of how important seeking is. I also hope you have an idea of what you want to seek. Here are a few final thoughts on the subject of seeking.

Determining what you should seek is not an easy task. It will involve finding out what you really desire and discovering what you are passionate about. It will require you to make good choices. In order to do all of this, you will need wisdom. The really good thing about wisdom is that God promises to give you all the wisdom you need, if you ask him for it. He also promises he will give it to you without reproach[59], which means he is not going to blame you for anything you did or haven't done before he gives you wisdom. It is like he is your daddy (Abba), and when you go to him asking for help in making a decision, he won't say things like, "Well, the last time you asked me, you really screwed it up, so forget you." Your Father does not do that, ever. His only condition is that when you ask him for wisdom, you don't doubt. When you get an answer, you can't doubt it is what you should do.

---

59 *The Holy Bible*, James1:5

I find that a lot of people will use words like knowledge, understanding, and wisdom interchangeably. They do not mean the same thing. *Knowledge* is pretty self-explanatory. It means knowing the truth. However, I would caution you to make sure you know the truth, and don't just assume something is true. Please remember to check your assumptions. *Understanding* takes knowledge one step further. Just because you know a truth does not mean that you really understand it and how it applies. Understanding means completely grasping all the aspects of a truth and the whole concept.

Wisdom is about being able to apply knowledge and understanding. Wisdom involves knowing the right thing to do in a given situation. Wisdom is not an intellectual property. Sometimes you can have enough experience in matters that you know what to do because you have seen the results from the same situations before. This is a form of wisdom. However, when you have not faced a situation before, and you need to know the right thing to do, you can ask for wisdom and receive it without reproach. You can count on the fact that as you seek, you will have many occasions when you won't know what to do. If you ask for wisdom in these situations you can rest easy, knowing you will get it.

Obviously, what you seek is your choice, but whatever it is, you should seek for more than just enough. There is an unlimited supply of wealth (money, love, relationships) in the world. Some people have the idea that seeking just enough for themselves is what they should do. Part of this comes from the idea that it is wrong to be rich, as I discussed previously. Some of it also comes from the idea there is only so much wealth out there, so if I have more than I need, then someone else won't have enough. That is simply not true. It might have been true during the Middle Ages, but not now. In fact, if you have the ability and the gift to create more than enough for yourself, and you choose not to, you are actually deciding to be selfish. There are a number of people and organizations that desperately need some of your abundance because they are hurting right now, and they don't know what you know. If you have the ability to create abundance, then I would tell you this: you will be able to help many more from your abundance than you could if you were in lack, or just getting by. The main reason we receive a gift is to be able to give it.

When it comes to seeking and asking for wisdom, I find myself back in the Bible for answers on these subjects. As I say that, I want to caution once again not to hear *religion* when I speak of the Bible. What I will talk about next is the *truth*. You have the choice to agree or disagree, to accept it as truth or not.

When talking about the subject of money, Saint Matthew records some very applicable things that Jesus said. I have five different versions of the Bible, and several reference books to help me understand what is really being communicated. My preferred version is the New American Standard Version. If that is not yours, I am in no way trying to get you to switch; I am only mentioning it for a good reason. In my Bible, before verse 25 of Matthew's chapter six, there is a title with these words: *The Cure for Anxiety*. I thought that was a very pertinent subject for almost everyone. I think you would have to agree there is a lot of anxiety in the world, today.

The Cure for Anxiety talks about what not to worry about. Jesus says we should not worry about what to eat, or drink, or what to wear. Basically, he is saying, in today's vernacular, "Stop worrying about money." He says the ungodly seek these things. They spend all of their efforts striving after, and thinking about, money. They are striving for money for survival, and for things they want. But here comes the good part. Jesus tells us, point blank, what we should seek. He says, "But seek first His Kingdom and His righteousness, and all these things will be added to you.[60]" This is a promise! He is saying that all the things we desire will be added to us, if we do it his way.

What does "seek first His kingdom and His righteousness" mean? How can you do this? It is a little difficult for an American to grasp the concept of a kingdom, because we think that the ultimate form of government is a democracy. Actually, even the United States is not a democracy; it is really a republic, but that is a different discussion. A good kingdom would be a much better form of government than a democracy or a republic. The problem is there has never been a "good" earthly kingdom. In a good kingdom, the king would be all wise, perfectly just, and always do what was best for his people. Because the king would be all wise and perfectly

---

60   *The Holy Bible*, Matthew 6:33

just, he would be the law, and his word would be final. As a Christian, this is the Government we are supposed to expect when Jesus returns at the Second Coming. So when Jesus tells us to seek first his kingdom, it means to seek his way of doing things in the perfect kingdom, in which God is the head, and all of the people do his will. Seeking first his kingdom also means seeking God's will because it is perfect for you.

His righteousness is even harder for us to grasp. Having understanding (as defined above) about God's righteousness is critical for any Christian. Righteousness means being able to stand before the Father without any condemnation. Since we have all sinned and fallen short of what the Father requires, we cannot be righteous on our own. This is where Jesus comes to our rescue, and why we call him Savior. When anyone breaks a law, there is a penalty associated with it. The penalty for sin, any sin, no matter how large or small, is death. To be righteous, you can have no sin. To stand in God's presence without any condemnation, you have to be spotless. No human can do that; it is impossible. In our humanity, it is an impossible quest. BUT, since Jesus is God, and is sinless, when he died for our sins, he paid the penalty we could never pay. Jesus chose to give us his righteousness as a gift. The gruesome punishment he accepted at the hands of the Romans paid your debt for every sin you ever committed, or ever will commit. His gift of righteousness does not have to be earned by us, just received. So, when we accept this gift of righteousness, we can actually go before the King of Kings and the Lord of Lords with no guilt or shame, because of what Jesus did for us. We can ask the Father for our desires without any condemnation. That concept is so radical, that most religious leaders will fight you to death over it. They fear that when you realize this is true, you will also realize you don't need them to mediate with God for you. And that is exactly right! Your Father wants you to have a relationship with Him, not some religious leader who wants to exert his power and influence over you.

So when Jesus said to seek first his kingdom and his righteousness, and all these things would be added to you, he wasn't kidding. The challenge is this: almost no one does it (seeks Jesus' kingdom and righteousness). The cares of this world, and its deceitfulness, distract us from seeking what we really should seek. The good news is that you are not condemned if you don't seek first His kingdom. You just miss out on all he has for you. It is your choice.

Chapter 24

Let's Get Real

Finding the answers you need can be a confusing process. It seemed that whenever I read a book, or listened to a speaker talk about subjects relating to my quest, the same two things would bother me.

First, I came away feeling I had only part of the picture. Second, I didn't really know what I was supposed to do next, or how to apply what I just learned. The result was that I got some good information, but my life didn't really change all that much. I was looking for real answers, and came away feeling empty and disappointed.

There are a lot of good books, written by very smart people, on some of the subjects covered in *The Holy Hand Grenade*. I have listed some of them for you in the section titled "Recommended Reading." There are also seminars and workshops you can attend to increase your knowledge in areas you may be particularly interested in. But to really get something that can change your life by reading *The Holy Hand Grenade*, you will need wisdom.

The wisdom I am referring to involves the ability to take the knowledge and understanding you have gained from reading, and be able to apply it. You will have to really spend some time meditating on what to do with this information. Unfortunately, telling you that you will need to do something on your own in order to make progress, never really goes over too big. But, that is why I think the third of the three questions is the most important. Seeking is crucial to finding.

Of course, if you aren't really seeking something, but only reading a book for pleasure, or because someone told you to do so, you can't expect much change, can you? So, I call this part of the book *Let's Get Real*, because it will help you apply what you have learned so far.

The reason I wrote *The Holy Hand Grenade* is because I have a vision for you. My vision is:

That you would realize you have been chosen and appointed by God; that you would know you have a seed of greatness in you, and that you would discover the desire and passion to develop that seed into its full potential.

Take Action

Don't settle for what you have right now. Regardless of how well you may be doing, I think you will have to admit there is room for more growth. You don't need to resign yourself to a life of quiet desperation. You can live life to the full. The keys to finding what you seek are desire and passion, and these can always be increased. If you don't know your desire, would like to have some passion for a change, or you already have some, but would like more, then there are a few things I recommend to you.

1. Did you take the personality profile test? If not, why not? Do it now. Go to www.thediscpersonalitytest.com and click on DiSC Reports. Take the DiSC Classic 2.0 Report for a twenty page report on your personality. It costs $29.00, and you can see an example of a report before you decide if you want to purchase the test. If you want greater detail on your personality I recommend the test at www.personalityinsights.com. Click on the Discovery report logo in the upper right of the page, and then click on *Need a Code* to take the Discovery Report - Adult Personality test, product code 3000, for $59.95.

a. Pay particular attention to the positive things it says about your personality and your value to organizations. Remember, not everyone has your personality. What you bring to an organization is quite unique. You shouldn't ignore your weaknesses, but most people tend to dwell on them. Do not spend time trying to fix areas that are not strengths as shown in your profile. Once you have taken the personality test, go back and read the whole book again. I promise you it will read differently. Do not read any further until you have done this! That's an order (just kidding…sort of).

2. Did you take the *Strengthsfinder 2.0* test? Same thing: If not, why not? This is part of seeking that is crucial to your success. No matter how successful you may be right now, if you focus more on your strengths, and delegate your weaknesses where possible, your effectiveness will soar. Focusing on your strengths will enable you to work more with passion than if you are spending your most valuable asset (time) on building up your weaknesses. It is good to recognize what your weaknesses are, so you don't get blindsided and so you can better relate to people, but most folks work so hard on their weaknesses that they never develop their strengths. The result is mediocrity. No one has a desire to be mediocre. Remember, the top strength in this test is your gift. So, if you haven't already taken the *Strenthsfinder* test, do it now! Get the book *StrengthsFinder 2.0* by Tom Rath. The code to take the online test is part of the book.

3. This part is optional, but it could be very helpful. Get Dr. Caroline Leaf's book *The Gift in You*. Take the Gift Profile test in her book to see how your brain functions best. For some people, discovering how their brain functions can give them some huge breakthroughs. Any edge you can get in determining how you operate best will be an asset in fulfilling your desire. There is one point of clarification in Dr Leaf's terminology and mine. Her book describes the particular way your brain functions as your gift. While I agree that how your brain functions is a unique part of who you are and is part of your gift, my definition is different.

The gift you have is the special thing you can do better than anyone else.

4. Did you discover your gift? If not, then taking your personality and your strengths into consideration, here are some hints for you:

   a. In what areas do your personality and your strengths line up?

   b. In your *Strengthsfinder* report, in Section I: Awareness for your top strength, in the section titled *What makes you stand out?*, what is it that sticks out the most to you? If someone else looked at your top strength, what do you think would stick out most to that person?

   c. In your *Strengthsfinder* report, in Section II: Application for your top strength, where it lists *Ideas for Action*, what really sticks out to you?

   d. Now, do the same thing for the other four strengths. Is there one thing that jumps out at you more than the rest? Is there one thing, if you could really do it, that would be very exciting and fulfilling to you? This report is telling you that you already have the gift to do it!!!

5. When you think about your gift, do you use your brain to its fullest capacity in using your gift? This is what Dr. Leaf's book is all about. Do you think best when you can lock yourself away in seclusion, or do you need music in the background to do your best thinking? Do you need to pace or walk around in order to think straight, or do you have to talk to think? However your brain is wired, it is a very good idea to go with it. Figure out how you think and spend some real quality time doing just that. If you have to lock yourself in a room with no distractions, then do it. If you have to go on a long walk or find someone to talk to as a sounding board, do it. You owe it to yourself. As Napoleon Hill said, "Think and Grow Rich." No one can do this for you.

6. Find a mentor.

Chapter 25

Mentorship

A MENTOR IS A TRUSTED COUNSELOR or guide according to the dictionary. But the etymology (the word history) of *mentor* has a much more interesting, and deeper meaning.

In Greek mythology, Mentor was the name of a person in the *Odyssey*, written by Homer. The Odyssey is the story about the travels of Odysseus after the Trojan War. Before Odysseus departed from Greece to fight in the war against Troy he put Mentor, an old and wise man, in charge of training his son, Telemachus. While Odysseus was on his odyssey, the goddess Athena wanted to provide divine counsel to Telemachus, so she appeared to him in the form of Mentor. While appearing as Mentor, it was actually the goddess Athena that showed Telemachus how to deal with the evil men that wanted to take his father's estate and possessions (his father, Odysseus, being too far away in Troy to defend his own property). Athena also appeared in the form of Mentor to Odysseus to give him wise counsel when he returned from his odyssey.

From this mythology, we see that a mentor is someone who imparts wisdom to, and shares knowledge with, a less experienced colleague. I find it interesting that the mythology also implies that Mentor's wisdom had a divine nature to it. Wisdom was imparted through Mentor's form, but it was Athena, the goddess of wisdom, who was actually providing the advice. This lines up very well with the discussion of wisdom in Chapter 23. Some people will tell you the best wisdom is experience, and you can certainly get wisdom from a trusted counselor who has experience in something you are going through. The best wisdom however, comes from God. Sometimes he will give it to you directly, and sometimes through a mentor.

Of the six recommendations for action, listed above, finding a mentor will be the most difficult. The biggest reason is that it will be difficult to know whom you can trust. The questions of who you really are, what your gift is, and what you seek are intensely personal and of the greatest concern. You can't just ask anyone to help you answer these questions. So, what should you look for in a mentor? The choice is yours, but this is what I look for:

1. Is the mentor living the way you want to live?
2. Does he know who he really is?
3. What is his gift?
4. What does he seek?
5. Does he have a vision which he is pursuing with passion?
6. Does he have any financial incentive in helping me? (The answer should be no)
7. Does he have experience in the areas I need answers?
8. Does he have his marriage together?
9. Is he financially responsible?
10. Does he have his emotions under control?
11. Who is his mentor?
12. Is he still growing mentally and spiritually?
13. What does he read?
14. Who does he associate with?
15. Are there any areas of his life that are out of control?

16. Does he have a Father fracture?
17. Is he guided by the Holy Spirit?

If you can find a mentor who fulfills your requirements for all of these questions, then you have found a really precious asset to your life. If, on the other hand, the person you call a mentor is shaky on any of these, you should be very careful about accepting that person's counsel. You cannot *assume* he has his act together on these questions, because that could be a bad assumption. A bad "mentor" can do much more harm than good. Even though finding a good mentor can be an asset, you are better off going it alone than getting advice from a questionable source.

Chapter 26

How and Where Do You Fit In?

GREATNESS COMES FROM USING YOUR gift in the place that you fit in. I almost said greatness comes from knowing where you fit in, but just knowing it doesn't help much. It is like the story of the three cats on a fence, mentioned earlier. They were making a lot of noise one night and woke up one of the neighbors, who opened his window and threw something at them. Two of the cats decided to get off the fence so they wouldn't get hit. How many cats were left? Answer: all three. Just deciding is not the same as actually getting off. Just knowing where you fit in is not the same as using your gift where you fit in. Neither is using your gift where you don't fit in.

There are people who are enormously gifted, and yet are completely wasting their lives. This usually happens because either they aren't using their gifts, or because they are using them in the wrong places. If you have a gift, and you know it, but you chose not to use it, then it doesn't do you any good. In this case, why aren't you using it? On the other hand, you could have an enormous gift, and be using it where it is not appreciated, and you will get the same effect—a wasted gift.

I am reminded of a You Tube video I saw of a cell phone salesman who was on a British version of American Idol. This guy, not looking like much of anything, appeared on stage in front of the judges. He needed to get his teeth fixed, he was a little pudgy, and he wasn't well dressed. The judges asked him what he was going to do, and he told them he was going to sing. Next, the judges asked him what he was going to sing, and the pudgy, toothless, sales guy said he was going to sing opera. The judges did everything they could not to burst out laughing. Then the guy opened his mouth to sing...and mesmerized the entire audience. When he finished, there wasn't a dry eye in the place because his voice was so moving. Here was a man with a great gift who was wasting his time as a cell phone salesman. The guy had little or no self-confidence, but at least he had the courage to show up for this competition.

I can't help wondering how many other people of equally great talents, with gifts that can benefit mankind, don't know where or how they fit in. There are entrepreneurs at heart who attempt to fit into someone else's corporation. That doesn't work. There are people whose peaks will be realized when working for the right corporation, but they try to start their own businesses. That doesn't work either. There are people who enter the ministry in order to hide from society, or for the money. That never works. There are people who get good grades in medical school and become doctors in order to fulfill their parent's desires, but they hate their jobs. That doesn't work either.

Finding your gift is awesome. Finding where to apply it is incredible. Actually, applying it where it fits is extremely gratifying. I have only found two places where someone describes how to find where and how to fit in. One is in business terminology: it is called a Master Mind. The other is in Christian terminology: it is called the Body of Christ.

The Master Mind is a principle Napoleon Hill wrote about. He found this principle by studying super wealthy business tycoons of the early 1900s. In Hill's terms, a Master Mind is formed when two or more people work in complete harmony toward a common definite purpose. The Master Mind group is comprised of people who have different, and non-competing gifts, who are coordinated and directed toward a common purpose. A Master Mind group forms a more complete pool of knowledge and talent, and is far more powerful, than any one of the members could form on his own. Hill says the Master Mind actually develops a third mind that is greater than the sum of all the minds added together[61].

I have never actually seen a business Master Mind at work, nor heard of one that exists today. There are several reasons that Master Minds are so difficult to create. First, trying to keep the members from competing with each other and trying to maintain harmony between business people is nearly impossible. There is also the problem of trying to find a purpose everyone agrees upon. If everyone doesn't benefit from the collective Master Mind it will break down. Hill received the basis of this principle from Andrew Carnegie. Carnegie tried to form Master Mind groups to operate his steel industry and found he had to replace all the members of the group at one time or another. I think the principle is sound, but the application is difficult. An option to the Master Mind that may work for you will be discussed in the next section on vision.

The concept of the Body of Christ was explained in Chapter 15. Unfortunately, just as with the Master Mind, I haven't seen the Body of Christ in operation, either. The reasons that the Master Mind principle hasn't really happened are the same reasons that the Body of Christ hasn't materialized yet. Members compete with one another; there is a lack of harmony; and everyone can't agree upon a common purpose. As soon as things begin to appear harmonious and unified, someone reveals his agenda, and the effort falls apart. This is not to say there aren't good churches, synagogues, etc. They just never seem to grow past a certain size without fracturing into different factions and taking on the detrimental aspects of religion. The Body of Christ is not just a sound principle, but it is what Christianity is supposed to be. As with the Master Mind principle, I think the main problem in fulfilling the Body of Christ has to do with vision.

---

61 *Law of Success*, Napoleon Hill

Chapter 27

Vision

So, figuring out how and where to fit in to use your gift can be difficult. In your seeking, if you happen to find a Master Mind, or find a church, synagogue, etc. where you can really use your gift to the fullest, then you have found a prize. For the rest of you, I have a suggestion. Find a cause or a vision that you really believe in and become a part of it.

Where there is no vision, the people perish.[62]

(Another translation of this proverb says, "where there is no vision, the people are unrestrained")

One of the core aspects of leadership is the gift of vision and being able to assemble a team to realize that vision. By vision, I don't mean someone who sees well, or someone who has mystical dreams. A leader with vision is someone who can see five or ten years into the future and know exactly what he wants his business or organization to look like. He can see where he wants to go, how he will get there, and the team that will be necessary to make it happen. A leader with vision gives those whom he is leading something greater to pursue. He gives them a mission that is bigger than

---

62 *The Holy Bible*, Proverbs 29:18

the group he leads. Someone who claims to be a leader, but does not have a clearly defined vision and a burning desire to fulfill it, is not really a leader, but merely a person occupying a leadership position. Sometimes people will refer to the person who is in charge as a leader, but more often than not, the so-called leader is actually a manager. Managers manage assets, whether they are numbers, products, or people. Leaders lead people by helping them reach their potential, and by directing their efforts toward a clearly defined purpose. Everyone wants to belong to something of value that is greater than him or her, and a leader with vision makes this possible.

There have been countless books written on leadership, and very few of the leaders they use as examples meet my definition of a leader. Leaders are born, not made. They have the gift of leadership from before they were born, but they can choose whether or not to develop that gift. A person who is not a born leader can rise to positions of authority, but that does not make him a leader. These kinds of so-called "leaders" never have the ability to inspire people to accomplish visions. When they attempt to inspire, their "inspiration" is more like goals and motivation, than inspiration to accomplish a vision. The amazing thing is that the people being led recognize a real leader and a vision, almost immediately.

Leadership belongs in business, the military, politics, sports, religion, and marriage. Unfortunately, the only groups that occasionally see leaders emerge seem to be found in the military and sports; but even there it is rare. The lack of leadership in business is mindboggling. Part of the Occupy Wall Street protest that occurred across the U.S. is the result of the lack of leadership in the business world. Leadership is about people and vision. Most businesses today are about the bottom line and reporting dividends to boards of directors. America has become so used to operating without real leadership and without vision that there is significant confusion and malaise. The people are literally perishing (unrestrained).

I recently had the privilege to speak with a prominent retired four-star general who now sits on as many as twenty different company boards of directors. I asked him what he thought the biggest problem in American business was today. Without any hesitation, he responded, "There is a general lack of excellence in America. If a forty percent effort is enough to get the bottom line that the board of directors wants, then that is what they get." This is a paraphrase from memory, and not a direct quote, but the general was extremely passionate about his answer. He went on to say that he felt as if nobody really cared whether their company was great, as long as the executives and the share holders got what they wanted. This was in stark contrast to the leadership he displayed and encouraged during his prestigious military career. The man was highly sought after in the business world for one reason: he is one of the rare leaders left in America.

Many times, people will refer to a coach as a leader. Sometimes, exceptional coaches are leaders, but leaders are not necessarily coaches. Most coaches understand the fundamentals of their sports, and they teach them to their players, while trying to execute a winning strategy for their teams. This, by itself, is not leadership. Leadership in sports involves a coach knowing the members of his team so well that he knows how to get more from each player than each player knew was possible. A leader-coach will get the full potential from each player and know how to employ his players to beat their opponents. Many times a leader-coach will be able to take a team with less raw talent than opposing teams and, through harmony and unity of purpose, mold his team into a finely tuned machine on the field.

If you haven't seen the movie *Blind Side*[63], based on Michael Lewis' book, I highly recommend it. A scene in the movie shows the coach having a hard time getting the main character of the movie to play well. This is a true story about Michael Oher, an NFL star lineman. In the scene, Michael is a huge African-American kid who has been abandoned by his parents but, through some very good fortune, winds up at a private Christian high school. Playing on a mostly white football team, Michael stands out because he is black, and because he is huge compared to other kids on his team. He seems like he would be a natural for football, but he has never played football before, and he is a gentle giant. While the coach is ready to give up on getting Michael to be aggressive on the field, his adopted mother in this movie, played by Sandra Bullock, marches out onto the practice field and starts giving Michael orders he can understand. Since Michael tested in the ninety-eighth percentile for protective instincts, she appealed to his desire to protect the quarterback, rather than appealing

---

63   *The Blind Side*, 2009, Warner Brothers

to him to crush the defensive player on the other side of the line. Well, it worked, and a superstar was born.

What is the point? The coach was not a leader. As Sandra Bullock struts off the practice field, she yelled back at the coach, "You need to get to know your players better, Earl." Earl got a lesson in leadership from one of the moms of his players.

Leadership in a marriage and family can be a touchy subject. But I can't leave this one alone. There are many very strong, confident women who have been born with leadership gifts. They should be the leaders in their homes, if their husbands are not born-leaders. Before some of you get your undies in a bundle, let me say this: the man in a marriage, even if his wife has more gifts of leadership, cannot surrender his responsibility in the relationship. Let me explain, please! Sometimes, the wife is the one who has the high D type personality, not the husband. This does not make her better than her husband, or make him weaker than his wife. It is just how they are wired. If both husband and wife were high D personalities, there would be a constant war to see who was going to lead. It would not look pretty. The old saying that opposites attract is true, and if the woman is the one with the high D, then the man will probably be more of an easy-going guy. Even in this case, it is still his responsibility to make sure the family and marriage function correctly.

There is a saying in the military that holds true in a marriage: you can delegate authority, but you cannot delegate responsibility. Any woman who takes the responsibility away from her husband is emasculating him, and it will not have a good end. I don't know why, but even in households where the woman clearly is the leader, she will follow her husband's vision for the family; if he doesn't abdicate it. The husband always has the responsibility for the family, but the authority to lead a family can be delegated to the wife, if she is the natural leader.

As you try to figure out where you fit in, and where to apply your gift, you need to consider this question: Do you have your own vision? I used to think everyone had a vision for their future. I was wrong. Can you imagine the chaos if every person was trying to fulfill a vision he created, and was looking for people to be on his team. In this scenario, the people you would be trying to recruit for your team would be trying to recruit you for their teams. It just wouldn't work. That is not to say you shouldn't have dreams for your future, but a vision is something much larger. People of vision imagine things on a grand scale and want to change things for the better. They see things as they could be, and ask, "Why not?" The vast majority of people do not think this way.

Do you have your own vision? Then you need others to fit into your plan. Leaders are not afraid or threatened by the greatness of their team members. Leadership brings out the greatness of others and gives that greatness places to be used. A visionary leader will actively seek smarter and more talented people than he is in order to make his vision a reality.

If you are not a person of vision (and that is most people), then you should find someone else's vision that you want to be a part of; but choose carefully whose vision you want to fit into. The one with the vision must see how you fit, and he must recognize the value you bring to the team. He must see it; not have you shove it down his throat. If he doesn't see it, then you probably do not belong in his plan. Your gift is just as valuable as the vision itself, because your gift will be a critical part of making that vision a reality. So, if you can't find a Master Mind or the Body of Christ functioning in your life, find a vision you can be part of. Your gift must be given in order for you to be really happy.

Chapter 28

Comparison, Part 2

Nothing can stop you in your tracks faster than comparison. We all tend to compare our weaknesses and shortcomings to others' strengths. The result is that you may think your gift is not as important as someone else's gift. The funny thing is that other people are also comparing themselves to you, thinking their gifts aren't as valuable as yours. It is precisely this kind of comparing that kills unity and harmony in an organization, and it is why strong leadership is required. A good leader will be able to detect when his people are feeling under-valued and beginning to compare themselves to others. He will emphasize their importance in the organization. He will help to understand their value—but he won't overdo it to the point that they feel more important than other team members.

When you know who you are and how you are wired, you can be free to be yourself. When you know your gift and develop it, you can be free of comparison and jealousy. You will be confident in where you are going and in the purpose for which you have been called. When you have that kind of confidence in yourself, you will be able to appreciate the gifts of others. You will begin to see how valuable other people's gifts are to the organization, and how without them your gift wouldn't function as well.

When everyone on the team knows who he is, what his gift is, and that he is doing his very best, everyone on the team will be free from envy, jealousy, guilt, and comparison. It will be okay with you if someone is great at something you are not good at. That is because you know you are great at something they aren't. You need each other in order to have all the bases covered. A company or organization that functions like this as much as possible will do things in excellence. I think this is what the four-star general was talking about. If you can keep your eyes off of yourself, and on to the purpose or vision, then great things happen.

Chapter 29

Purpose

"Until thought is linked with purpose there is no intelligent accomplishment. With the majority the bark of thought is allowed to "drift" upon the ocean of life. Aimlessness is a vice, and such drifting must not continue for him who would steer clear of catastrophe and destruction.

They who have no central purpose in their lives fall an easy prey to petty worries, fears, troubles, and self-pityings, all of which are indications of weakness, which lead, just as surely as deliberately planned sins (although by a different route), to failure, unhappiness, and loss, for weakness cannot persist in a power-evolving universe.

A man should conceive of a legitimate purpose in his heart and set out to accomplish it. He should make this purpose the centralizing point of his thoughts. It may take the form of a spiritual ideal, or it may be a worldly object, according to his nature at the time being; but whichever it is, he should steadily focus his thought forces upon the object which he has set before him. He should make this purpose his supreme duty, and should devote himself to its attainment, not allowing his thoughts to wander away into ephemeral fancies, longings, and imaginings.⁶⁴"

When you know what you seek, and you begin the journey to pursue it, you have purpose and focus in your life. Everything you do, the things you want, and even the entertainment you choose will relate to what you seek. Instead of trying to keep yourself amused so you don't have to deal with the dissatisfaction in your life, having purpose in all you do will actually bring you the joy you seek.

When you have a definite purpose in your life it is almost as if you grow antennas. Wherever you go and whatever you do, your antennas are automatically tuned to receive and evaluate what is going on around you, based on your purpose. What you think and how you evaluate information goes through the mental filter of your purpose.

My wife, Mary, is a health and nutrition fanatic. She thoroughly enjoys giving seminars on nutrition and health related issues. She is passionate about helping people lose weight and overcome disease. She works with women on hormonal issues. Whenever we go anywhere, her passion will come up in her conversation. She will notice someone who is obese and talk about how much she would like to help that person, or she will look at a woman's face and instantly know she is battling hormonal issues. When we go out to a restaurant, I call her the food Nazi—affectionately, of course. Fat, preservatives, body type, blood type, etc., etc., etc. are evaluated in her every menu and grocery store choice. She really can't help it; health is her passion.

"Without Purpose, abuse is inevitable." I stole that line from Dr. Creflo Dollar in a sermon he gave in Chicago. I am not sure if he coined the phrase, but the first time I heard him say it, the saying stuck with me. It really is true that if you don't have purpose in your life, you will end up abusing something. It could be your spouse or children; it could be alcohol or drugs; it could be pornography; or it could be something as innocuous as watching too much TV or playing too many video games. In Mary's case, she sees people who abuse food as destroying their health. All of these are abuses of some kind that have a detrimental effect on your life.

---

64 *As a Man Thinketh,* James Allen

When you have purpose, and the passion that goes with it, a kind of peace enters your life. That is because your purpose, the thing you seek, fills a void in your life that temporary pleasures cannot. Whenever I see someone constantly seeking pleasure, I immediately know they have not found what they seek. By itself, pleasure is not necessarily bad, but constantly seeking pleasure is a waste of your life. It never lasts and only causes you to seek more pleasure. Once you have purpose in your life, the desire for temporary pleasure is replaced with the happiness that comes from doing what you were created to do.

The first time I read the following passage I thought the guy was nuts. I think part of why I felt that way was because I wasn't used to hearing people talk (or write) about desire and obsession as good things. It is uncanny how accurate Hill's statement becomes to you once you have found your purpose.

"Your major responsibility, right now, is to find out what you desire in life, where you are going, and what you will do when you get there. This is one responsibility which no one but you can assume, and it is the responsibility ninety-eight out of every hundred people never assume. That is the major reason why only two out of every hundred people can be rated as successful.

Success begins through Definiteness of Purpose!

If this fact has seemed to be over-emphasized, it is because of the common trait of procrastination which influences ninety-eight out of every hundred people to go all the way through life without choosing a Definite Major Purpose.

Singleness of purpose is a priceless asset—priceless because so few possess it.

Yet, it is an asset which one may appropriate on a second's notice.

Make up your mind what you desire of life, decide to get just that, without any substitutes, and lo! you will have taken possession of one of the most priceless assets available to human beings.

But your desire must be no mere wish or hope!

It must be a burning desire, and it must become so definitely an obsessional desire that you are willing to pay whatever price its attainment may cost. The price may be much or it may be little, but you must condition your mind to pay it, regardless of what the cost may be.

The moment you choose your Definite Major Purpose in life you will observe a strange circumstance, consisting in the fact that ways and means of attaining that purpose will begin immediately to reveal themselves to you.

Opportunities you had not expected will be knocking at your door.

The cooperation of others will become available to you, and friends will appear as if by a stroke of magic. Your fears and doubts will begin to disappear, and self-reliance will take their place.[65]"

---

65 *The Master Key To Riches*, Napoleon Hill

Chapter 30

Competition versus Creativity

This subject of competition versus creativity is going to be controversial and will probably challenge some of your preconceived ideas. Most Americans have been taught that competition is good. In many ways our society is centered on competition. We almost idolize sports teams because of their abilities to compete. We highly regard businesses that are competitive, and say how good competition is for keeping prices low. Even churches get into competitive bouts by tracking numbers in their congregations and seeing how many conversions they can record.

Competition stems from an idea that there is not enough of something, so there is a need to compete for your share. In sports, this is generally true. There are only so many games in a season, and only so many teams in the playoffs, so there can be only one winner. The idea that there can be only one winner in a business situation is archaic. In days of old, when knights were bold, etc. you may have been able to make a case for that idea. There was only so much land and gold in a kingdom, so if you wanted more, you had to wage war to take it from someone else.

Today's concept of market share harkens back to that idea. In a given market, each business ends up competing for its share. But this idea would only be valid if the market was limited in its size. In today's world, assuming that a market size is limited is not always true. If your business enters a market that is already established, and your plan is to take a portion of what someone else has developed, then you are certainly in competition. Any plan for trying to succeed by taking something from someone else can only expect limited success.

Much of the greed in the world comes from the worldview that only limited amounts of resources or money are available. Because of this view, people get the idea that if someone is rich, he got that way at the expense of someone else. As in the Robin Hood legend, some people think the only way to help the poor involves taking goods from the rich. If money and wealth were limited, they might have a point; but they aren't limited. There was an urban legend circulating in 1899 that the commissioner of the U.S. Patent office was going to resign because "everything that could be invented was already invented." Even though this was just a legend, it does show how people can think resources and ideas are limited.

People who have learned to use their creativity realize they have tapped into an unlimited resource. There was an energy crisis in the 1850s. Whale hunting had seriously depleted the number of whales that could be harvested for the production of oil for lamps. Prices shot up and panic ensued. What were people to do? Someone used his creativity, and coal oil started to enter the market, followed by petroleum products, followed by electricity, and so on. Much of our reliance on petroleum products today, is a fabrication. It is a form of greed used by those who don't want to move on to much more efficient and less costly forms of energy. You can be quite confident that solutions to our energy needs already exist through someone's creativity, but those solutions are being kept quiet, for now.

There is probably not a person who was born in the U.S. that has not heard that mankind was created in the likeness and image of God. Many people don't want to put a name on God, for fear of being "intolerant," but calling him "the Creator" seems to be acceptable by most Americans. The nature of the Creator is to create, to cause that which did not previously exist to come into existence. Since we were created in his image, we are also supposed to create. How and what you create depends on who you are and what your gift is. The question for you is this: What can you create?

When you create something from your gift, you have something that has value you did not take away from someone else. This is your source of wealth. Instead of looking for ways to be competitive, try seeking to create something. You will be amazed at how you can create something from nothing, just by thinking about it. When you put passion behind your creation, don't be surprised to find that the resources you need to make it a reality will just start showing up. But remember, passion means keeping your antennas up at all times for things that relate to your desire. You cannot be casual about your creation, and your passion needs to be burning all the time if you want to make it a reality. Creativity trumps competition every time.

"To become really rich (a richer, fuller, more abundant life) is the nobelist aim you have in life, for it includes everything else. On the competitive plane, the struggle to get rich is a Godless scramble for power over other men; but when we come to the creative mind, all this is changed…

Moral and spiritual greatness is possible only to those who are above the competitive battle for existence; and only those who are becoming rich on the plane of creative thought are free from the degrading influences of competition. If your heart is set on domestic happiness, remember that love flourishes best where there is refinement, a high level of thought, and freedom from corrupting influences; and these are to be found only where riches are attained by the exercise of creative thought, without strife or rivalry.[66]"

---

66 *The Science of Getting Rich*, Wallace Wattles

PART V

Application

Chapter 31

I.C.I.—Applying your gift

A FEW YEARS AGO I HAD the privilege to hear Oral Roberts' last public sermon. I don't know what you think of Oral Roberts, but I remember thinking in my youth that he was a wacky "faith healer." My family didn't believe in his kind of ministry, and I even remember making fun of him and other such "weirdoes."

As I sat in a very packed church listening to Oral Roberts preach his last sermon, I no longer thought he was a "weirdo." He talked about a lot of things that day, but his description of the last time he literally heard God talk to him had me on the edge of my seat. He told us there were three times in his life he audibly heard God talk to him, and he felt the last conversation would have the greatest impact on this generation. Whether you believe he really heard this message from God or not, is your choice. But I think what he had to say about this last "conversation" will help you understand how to apply your gift.

The book of Malachi, which means *My Messenger*, is the last book of the Old Testament in the Bible. It was written about 430 B.C., during a time when the Jewish people were suffering from drought and famine, and had forgotten God. Verse 10 of chapter three is often quoted by preachers who talk about the importance of tithing—the practice of giving God a tenth of all your increase (earnings). While Oral Roberts certainly believed in the principle of tithing, he had a different message from God about this book in the Bible. In the tenth verse, the prophet Malachi is speaking God's words:

"Test Me now in this, says the Lord of hosts, if I will not open for you the windows of heaven and pour out for you a blessing until it overflows.[67]"

No matter who you are, or what you believe, if the windows of heaven opened up to pour out a blessing for you that overflowed, I'll bet you would take it! In fact, an overflowing blessing from heaven is what a lot of people hope and pray for. That is what Oral Roberts said God spoke to him about. He pointed out that God revealed that he would pour out a (singular) blessing, not blessings. He said God got very specific with him as to what that blessing was, and it was a message for this generation. Each person who met the conditions of this verse would receive the blessing of an Idea, a Concept, or an Insight that would be so powerful, the results of implementing it (or them) would cause overflow of abundance in that person's life. He went on to say that most people mistakenly expect God to shower them with gold or money from out of heaven, but it doesn't work like that. He will bless you with an *Idea, Concept,* or *Insight* (ICI) that would result in abundance in your life. This is a way of being creative instead of competing.

Ideas, according to Oral Roberts, come from the thought that you can do something different than what you have always done. When looking for a solution to increase their circumstances, most people only look in the areas of what they have always done, or are familiar with. Subconsciously, these people seriously limit their possibilities. The speed with which the world is changing from an industrial age to an information age makes it necessary that you remain open to ideas you may have no experience with. If you get an idea, don't let the thought that you can't do it, or don't know how to do it, enter your mind. Your thoughts of what you can't do could kill a perfectly good idea. Look at what you can do, instead. Can you check it out? Can you find someone who might be able to help you?

---

67 *The Holy Bible*, Malachi 3:10

Are there parts of the idea you can do now? Does the idea work well with your personality and gift?

Another killer of ideas is what I call "golden handcuffs." This is where you may have a job or profession that pays your bills, or even provides a nice lifestyle, but it is a job you really dread going to every day. You may have invested years of effort and education in order to be able to perform this job, only to find out it is not your dream. The fact that it provides you with a good lifestyle keeps you from taking the risk to pursue what you really want. You feel handcuffed to your job or profession, like you can't escape from it, even if you wanted to. Part of the reason for being "handcuffed" may also be because other people expect you to be in that profession. You are trapped by what others want you to do. I have met medical doctors who, after all their training, find out they don't like being physicians, but they feel trapped. The idea you get from God—excuse me, the Creator—may be to escape the golden handcuffs and to live the life you were destined for.

Concepts are completely new and original ideas. No one has done this, thought of this, or produced this before. God will not give you a concept without giving you the resources to make it a reality. But remember, you will probably not be able to do it on your own. Also, don't let your concept be stolen by the thought "if this could work, then someone else would have already thought of it", or "who are you to come up with a great concept?" Actually, who are you NOT to come up with new concepts? Why not you?

Insights are ways of looking at things that already exist, but looking at them from different angles. You may realize your gift is to be able to see things others miss. You may get an insight as to how a product can be used for an entirely new application. In today's economic environment, any product that is already being manufactured but that can be used in a new application would be worth a substantial amount to most manufacturers. Your insight could also mean you take something deeper than has been done in the past—the current applications for which you have insight may have just scratched the surface of what you see as possible.

I think the point Oral Roberts was making is that you need to expect to get great thoughts that can be creatively turned into tangible blessings.

The thought, in the form of an idea, a concept, or a new insight, is God's blessing to you; a means of honoring you for fulfilling his desire. How you apply an idea, concept, or insight you are given will depend on your gift. You will not receive a blessing you cannot fulfill. Your ICI will fit perfectly with who you are, and what you desire. When you get a thought that comes to you from out of the blue, a thought that could be a blessing poured out from heaven, don't ignore it. Write it down; explore it as a possibility, and talk it over with your mentor. Take action on it, because it is your creativity that will produce what you are looking for.

Chapter 32

Ambush

You may find that just about the time you start to figure out who you really are, what your gift is, and what you seek, something comes along and blindsides you. It knocks you off track and makes you want to give up. I call this being ambushed, and this is when you need more firepower—a Holy Hand Grenade.

While I was stationed at Camp Pendleton, California, there was a story circulating about an infamous ambush on the base. It seems a platoon of Marines was practicing night ambushes on a warm southern California night. They had set up machine guns with blank ammunition at both ends of the ambush site. They also set popup flares and explosive noise making devices to simulate Claymore mines. The idea was to create the ambush site, and then ambush other aggressor Marines (dressed up as bad guys), who would walk down the path at a predetermined time during the night.

As some of you may know, Southern California has some issues with illegal aliens crossing the border. It just so happens that one of the U.S. Customs and Border Patrol checkpoints is on Interstate 5 where it cuts through Camp Pendleton. Sometimes illegal aliens will get out of their vehicles somewhere south of the checkpoint, walk through Camp Pendleton, and then get back in their vehicles, somewhere north of the checkpoint.

As the night grew darker, and the coastal fog started to roll in, one of the Marines in the ambushing platoon heard some movement. The platoon was quietly alerted that the aggressors were approaching their "kill zone." (A "kill zone" is where the ambushers have carefully planned their fire so that as many bad guys are killed as possible). As the aggressors entered the "kill zone," one of them tripped the popup flare. As soon as that happened, both machineguns started firing and the Claymore mines were detonated. Then, all the Marines in the ambush platoon started firing rifles loaded with blanks.

Unfortunately the aggressors in the kill zone weren't the Marines who were dressed as bad guys. Apparently, a group of illegal aliens had wandered into the area where the Marines were practicing ambushes. I would be willing to bet there were some soiled pants in that group of illegals. After making it all the way across the border, and about fifty miles inside the U.S., they probably thought they were almost home free—then to be ambushed by Marines at night! Can you imagine the shock they must have been in?

As a new Marine lieutenant at the Basic School, I was taught how to ambush bad guys, as well as what to do if ambushed. If you are ambushed, you can bet your enemy has chosen very carefully where he will spring the ambush. His plan is to keep you in the "kill zone," the area where he has preplanned his fire in order to inflict, for as long as possible, the most damage on you. The longer you stay in that zone, the less likely it is that you will get out alive. If you have to think about what you are going to do after you are ambushed, there is a great likelihood you aren't going to make it. That is why we practiced "Immediate Action" drills. Immediate Actions are what you do, without having to think, if you get ambushed. Even though lying down to take cover is the most natural thing to do, we were taught to face the fire and attack through it. Now, if you have to think about it, you are never going to do that in a real ambush. But, if you practice it over, and over, until it becomes habit, you just might actually do it. I don't know what they teach for Immediate Action drills now, but whatever they teach, Immediate Action drills can save your life in a combat situation.

The same holds true for you. When you discover who you are, your gift, and what you seek, don't be surprised if you get ambushed. Your ambush could come in the form of your job being cut. It could come from someone who is jealous of your newfound confidence. It could come in the form of "Who do you think you are?" comments from people you love and trust. It could come from evaluating what you thought were truths, only to find out that they were assumptions, and they were wrong. In any case, if you get ambushed, you will need to know your Immediate Action drills. As I described previously, you can't afford to make up these immediate actions while you are in the middle of an ambush. You need to make your immediate actions now, and practice them until they become habit. That way, when someone, or something, comes against you, you will know what to do.

Here are some suggestions for your Immediate Action drills:

1. Get out of the ambush. If it is someone who is doing the ambushing, get away from him or her as quickly and politely as possible. Do not argue with that person. As it says in *How To Win Friends and Influence People* by Dale Carnegie, "The only way to get the best of an argument is to avoid it.[68]"

2. Write out your "I Am" statement and keep copies of it with you wherever you go. Repeat it out loud to yourself several times a day until it becomes a habit.

3. If you have a mentor, call him as soon as you are ambushed. You can't do this every time you feel sorry for yourself, but when you are ambushed your mentor can help you get up and out of the kill zone. There is a caveat here: you have to determine before the ambush that you will do what the mentor says. During an ambush is not the time to think about it.

4. Assuming you have figured out how you think the best, use your best way of thinking to get out of the ambush. If you need motion, then go for a walk. If you need quiet, then lock yourself in a room with a "do not disturb" sign on the door. If you need music, put your headphones on and blast yourself with your music

---

68 How to Win Friends and Influence People, Dale Carnegie

Chapter 33

Examples

MANY PEOPLE CAN READ BOOKS that tell them all the steps to take but never really get anything out of them. One of the reasons for this is that some people learn better by doing rather than by having someone tell them how to do something. My own experience is that I learn best by someone giving me an example to follow. Since the variations of personalities, gifts, ways of thinking, etc. can be plentiful, I have provided four examples for you that cover each of the main personality types and a variety of other factors. The examples are fictitious, so if one of them sounds like you, or someone you may know, it is merely a coincidence.

Example 1: Dan

Dan grew up in the suburbs of Washington, D.C. He had a better-than-middle class upbringing due to his father's job as a government employee in the Defense business. Dan's father had a doctorate in strategic analysis. He taught Dan to do well in school so he could go to the right college. His father had visions of Dan following in his footsteps, with an advanced degree and a secure job in the government.

Dan's mother was outgoing and vivacious. She was the life of the party and a bit of a risk-taker. She was the exact opposite of Dan's father, who was extremely cautious and conservative. At first, their differences made them interesting to each other, but as Dan's father became more involved in his job and less involved at home, the marriage fell apart. When Dan was 17, his parents divorced.

Dan exhibited the intelligence of his father but the outgoingness of his mother. He and his dad never really got along, and Dan thought his father was a loser. Dan was a natural athlete, a leader on the field and self-reliant. Dan regarded his father as a bit of a nerd, and saw that his father let his mother lead at home.

Dan chose to study engineering in college. His overwhelming desire to achieve demanded he do well in whatever he chose. So, even though he had no real affection for engineering, he finished at the top of his class. The only reason he chose engineering was to appease his father, plus Dan didn't know what else he would study instead. In college, he found he did not need a lot of sleep, and was awake most mornings well before his fraternity brothers even thought of getting up. Dan served as the head of his fraternity, ran for several other student organizations and, as he expected of himself, eventually led all of them.

After graduation, a Fortune 500 aerospace company offered Dan a position. Very impressed with Dan's college record, the company proposed to pay for an advanced degree if he signed on. The excitement of having his first job and making money only lasted a year. Working for a huge corporation carried some prestige with it, but Dan began to feel he was just one of thousands in the organization. Whenever he submitted innovative solutions to projects he worked on, they were shot down. The mantra "That's not how we do things here!" really started to eat at his drive to create. After a year and a half with the corporation, Dan's boss called him into his office for the first job appraisal Dan received since he began working at the company. Dan's boss told Dan he thought Dan was an extremely diligent and bright worker, but that Dan's forceful and strong-willed demeanor had caused some ill feelings with his coworkers. Dan's boss advised him to learn to not rock the boat, and to go with the flow.

The boss advised Dan that if he followed that advice, he would have a very promising, long-term future at the corporation.

Dan let his boss' advice sink in for six months. During that time, Dan ran into Claire at work. Claire had been a year ahead of Dan when they attended the same college, and they knew each other from some classes they had taken together. Claire was new at the corporation, having recently left a small engineering firm where she had worked for two years. Dan asked Claire if she would meet him for coffee to discuss work. When they met, Dan told her how frustrated he was with all the procedures and how long it took to get anything done at the corporation. In his eyes, there didn't seem to be any innovation or creativity there. Claire told him she had just left a small start-up engineering firm. Her experience with the small firm was that they had no procedures, and they were too creative. She did not understand why Dan didn't love working at the corporation. In Claire's mind, the corporation was just what an engineering company was supposed to be like.

Dan took Claire's and his boss' counsel to heart. He realized that his current position was not what he really wanted. The problem was that he didn't know what he really wanted. He started looking for career options. He knew he was destined to do great things, and it seemed as if he had run into a roadblock. Not knowing where to begin, he fell back on what had worked for him in the past. As he learned in college, when all else fails, throw a party.

Dan called some of his fraternity brothers and organized a tailgate party for an upcoming college football game. Everyone showed up and had a great time. Dan completely forgot about his dilemma and was just glad he could be himself around old friends. He didn't have to worry about overpowering anyone or watching his P's and Q's when he spoke about his aspirations and frustrations. It turned out that his best friend had been going through some of the same things. The friend was surprised that Dan couldn't turn his situation around merely by the force of his personality. Dan's friend said he had just read a book called *The Holy Hand Grenade*, which dealt with their exact situations. He recommended the book to Dan and suggested that Dan take the different tests recommended in the book.

Dan wasn't just playing around. True to his nature, he wanted to find a solution to his career issues. Dan read *The Holy Hand Grenade* and took the tests. Here is what he found out.

Dan's Personality profile: a high D personality with a Developer pattern.

His goals are centered on new opportunities. He fears boredom and loss of control. His value to an organization is his innovative problem-solving methods. He is self-reliant, strong-willed, forceful, focused on results and can lack empathy.

Dan's Strength: Achiever

Dan's strength is his need for achievement. He is driven, would work every day if he could, and is self-motivated. Because more work is exciting to him, Dan needs a job that allows him to work as hard as he wants.

He is a Kinesthetic Thinker

Dan is always in motion. His constant movement can drive his coworkers crazy, so a coach recommended he sit on a big ball instead of a chair when he is at a desk.

Dan's Father Fracture grew when his parents divorced.

Dan's father never understood Dan's super-achieving desires and his willingness to take risks. Dan thought there was something wrong with him because he was not more like his father. Dan thought his dad was a bit of a loser (though he still wanted his dad's approval), and he never felt approved by his dad.

His Love language: Words of affirmation

When someone tells him how awesome he is, especially if it is someone he trusts, Dan feels loved. His mother filled that void for him by telling him how proud she was of him. His high school football coach also affirmed Dan, and the coach and he still have a strong mentorship bond.

Based on this new information Dan realized who he really was. He also realized his desire to achieve was not because he was fanatical workaholic; it was because achieving was his strength. He reconnected with his high school football coach and found him to be an excellent mentor. In one of their mentoring sessions, his coach realized Dan had wanted to design specialty cars since Dan was a kid. He even won an engineering design competition for a new engine during his senior year in college. Dan hadn't realized how much of a passion car-designing was for him until he took a step back, and until his mentor showed him how much of Dan's life had centered on cars.

Dan decided he would go into the automobile-design business for himself. Based on good counsel, he planned to leave his Fortune 500 position after he had his finances and plans in order. He also knew he needed to keep his plans to himself for a while, so he could leave his employment on his terms. Dan's whole outlook seemed brighter, and he could not have been more excited about his future.

Example 2: Isabel

Isabel came from a happy middle-class family in Texas. Her father worked in a warehouse, and her mother stayed home with the five children; Isabel was the middle child. Isabel's father was always happy and everyone's friend. Isabel was much like her father.

Isabel's father was killed in a work accident when she was seven years old. Overnight, her family's situation went from happy to sad and depressed. The family had to move to a poorer neighborhood and try to live on the income her mother could provide and the meager insurance they received from her father's accident. Isabel still maintained her cheerful disposition in school and with her friends, but life with four siblings, in a poor neighborhood, was tough on her. She vowed to herself not to live that way when she grew older.

After high school graduation, Isabel decided to become an accountant. She knew accountants were always in demand, and the steady income appealed to her need for some kind of financial security. She did not ask her mother's advice about careers, mainly because her mother was too busy trying to raise Isabel's younger brothers and sisters, but also because her mother had never been very supportive of Isabel.

There was only one thing wrong with being an accountant: Isabel hated it. She was talkative and energetic while all the other accountants were quiet and boring. She liked to have fun; they liked numbers. She liked talking to clients; they only wanted to stay in their cubicles. Isabel didn't like telling her friends what she did for a job, because she felt they might think it wasn't very cool.

It didn't take long for Isabel to figure out she had chosen the wrong profession. The problem was she didn't know what the right profession was. To make matters worse, she had no idea how to find out. One thing was for sure: there was no way she was going to jeopardize the financial security her income provided. Quitting without a solid job offer from the "right" profession was not an option for her. She had a huge social network, so she asked her Facebook friends for advice about career opportunities. One of her friends Facebooked back that she should be careful about what she was asking on Facebook because it wasn't difficult for companies to find that information. Isabel's response was that the people in her office didn't really have any friends, and that Facebook was the last place they would ever look. In this case, she was right. She was also careful not to say anything bad on her Facebook comments about where she worked.

One of Isabel's real friends (as opposed to her Facebook friends) suggested she read *The Holy Hand Grenade*. Her friend Jennifer recommended it because of the section on the Father Fracture. Jen knew how much Isabel missed her father and thought her reading that section might help. Reluctantly, Isabel read it, and with prodding from Jennifer, she took the tests. Isabel was pleasantly surprised.

Isabel's Personality profile: a high I personality with a Persuader pattern.

Her goals are focused on authority and prestige, and a Persuader likes status symbols. She is afraid of complex relationships, and the thought of not being able to have a change of environment makes her anxious. Her friendly, outgoing and enthusiastic personality, along with her poised and confident manner, enables her to close sales effortlessly. She would be of great value to any sales organization. She wants to look good at work, likes multiple activities, and draws people to her.

Isabel's strength: Positivity

Her enthusiasm is contagious and people wish their glasses were as a full as hers. Isabel injects drama into all she does. She is light-hearted and generously praises those around her. Her presence reminds people that it is good to be alive.

She thinks Interpersonally.

If Isabel needs to make a decision, she will usually turn to the people she trusts (which is almost everyone) and ask their advice. While it might appear she does not have an opinion of her own, that is incorrect. Other peoples' opinions help her decide if she is right.

She knew she had a Father Fracture; she just didn't know what it was called. The loss of her father was devastating to her. The Father Fracture information in *The Holy Hand Grenade* helped her realize she felt abandoned by her father, and that it affected her naturally trusting attitude. She now knew why she was afraid of getting too close to someone—because they might leave her. Being afraid of being abandoned affected her spiritual life as well. All of this new knowledge helped Isabel trust people, and trust God, as she had when she was little.

Isabel's Love Language: Gifts

When someone gives her a gift, she feels especially appreciated. It doesn't even matter how big or expensive the gift is or whether she likes it or not. To Isabel, it really is the thought behind the gift. After reading about the Father Fracture, Isabel enjoyed a wonderful conversation with her mother, who gave Isabel her father's cross necklace as a token of her love for Isabel. Isabel couldn't stop crying for a week.

Three weeks after Isabel met with her mother (in other words, two weeks after she stopped crying), the owner of a training company visited the accounting firm where Isabel worked. That man, John, needed some tax work done, and Isabel's supervisor asked if Isabel would mind showing John around until his paperwork was ready. After just five minutes of walking John through the firm, he stopped her dead in her tracks and asked her what she did at the firm. When Isabel told him she was an accountant, John burst out laughing. He just gave her his card and said he would give her a call regarding his business.

The following week, John called Isabel at her workplace and asked if she had time to meet him at his office. Her firm had no issues with it, so Isabel followed through with the meeting, not really knowing what to expect. John apologized for the secrecy, but told her he had spoken to her boss and wanted to hire her as a salesperson for his training company. After John described the proposed position and the salary, and after Isabel met some of the people at John's company, she jumped at the opportunity. Selling and training people is what she had always wanted to do, and the increased salary she was offered made the timing right for Isabel.

Example 3: Stephen

Stephen, the son of farming parents, comes from a small Midwest town. He grew up with a stable family situation and had an uneventful childhood. He played the normal sports in high school and got okay grades. During his senior year, Stephen decided to leave "Smalltown, U.S.A." and see the world, so he enlisted in the Navy. He was selected to become a Corpsman—the Navy's version of a medic.

When Stephen finished his medical training, he was stationed in California with a Marine Corps unit. At twenty years of age, he found himself in Afghanistan, serving alongside Marines in the thick of combat. This was not exactly what he had in mind when he left the farm to see the world, but since he was there, he decided to make the best of it. When he wasn't saving Marines lives by providing emergency medical treatment on the battlefield, he found himself trying to save them from killing each other back at their base. Stephen only thought his buddies back home were rowdy; they were no comparison to these Marines. These Marines were the best friends he ever had. He felt closer to them than to his own brother.

After serving his four-year enlistment, Stephen had had enough of seeing the world, and longed for home. From his old local community, he received a hero's welcome, partly because he had received some press from the Navy after he won a medal for valor in combat. His mom couldn't stop hugging and kissing him as he walked in the front door on returning home. His dad shook his hand, and for the first time in Stephen's life, told him how proud he was of his son. His dad was not an emotional man, and could not bring himself to hug the son he thought so much of.

After decompressing from the military for about a month, Stephen set out to find a job. The poor economy had hit his hometown pretty hard, and jobs were difficult to come by. He finally found a position selling cars at the local Chevy dealership. Stephen didn't know for sure, but he thought the dealership owner felt sorry for him and gave him the job because of his "celebrity "status. It certainly wasn't because Stephen was a salesperson. He went to work every day and gave it his best, but Stephen detested selling. He just didn't know what else he could do.

Some of his friends stayed in the Marine Corps, but most of them got out after their commitments. Stephen stayed in touch with all of them on Facebook and helped to keep their camaraderie alive. It was through one of his Facebook conversations that he learned from a friend about *The Holy Hand Grenade*. Stephen read the book twice and took all the tests. He was feeling a little desperate to make something of his life and hoped this would give him some answers. Here is what he found out.

Stephen's Personality profile: a high S personality with a Specialist pattern.

His personality wants to have a controlled environment, and he likes to go with the status quo. He is fearful of disorganization and change. His value to any organization is that he is steady, predictable and consistent. He will bend his will to accommodate others, and he works well with almost all other personalities. The biggest way he judges people is through friendship. He is patient, considerate, and always willing to help.

Stephen's Strength: Harmony

Stephen doesn't like conflict; in fact, he steers people away from confrontation. He won't even discuss controversial issues with people because it bothers him so much. The group's desires are always more important to him than his own desires. He genuinely likes people and will build networks to communicate with them. He wants everyone to be heard, and will strive to find common ground between people in order to stop disputes. He is a peacemaker.

He is a Musical Thinker: Stephen got hooked on light jazz in San Diego when he was stationed with the Marines (Camp Pendleton being only forty miles north of San Diego). He listens to music to keep himself calm and to think through problems. You will find him with an iPod permanently fixed to his ears.

Father Fracture: Until Stephen read the section in *The Holy Hand*

Grenade about the Father Fracture, he would have told you he had a great relationship with his father. He discovered a clue that it wasn't as good as he thought it was when he came back from the Navy and his father couldn't even give him a hug. To this day, Stephen has never heard his father tell him he loves him.

His Love language: Acts of service

When someone goes out of his way to do something for him, Stephen feels especially appreciated. After a particularly difficult patrol in Afghanistan, in which Stephen went through almost all of his medical supplies working on wounded Marines, a couple of the guys spent three hours scrounging supplies for his medical kit. They were all exhausted, and had their own duties to take care of before they went back out, but his Marine buddies put Stephen first. He never forgot that.

After finding out who he really was, Stephen knew why selling was not for him. What he really wanted was to be part of a team that mattered. He enjoyed being around a group of people who were engaged in doing something significant, and he had a real knack for emergency medicine. So Stephen enrolled in Emergency Medical Services (EMS) courses, using the money he received from his military service. He became a qualified EMS paramedic with the local Fire Department. When a city located twenty miles away found out he had been a Navy Corpsman working with Marines in Afghanistan, they offered him a position on their SWAT unit.

Stephen found working with the SWAT unit had similarities with his Navy experience—but without as much stress as combat. He thoroughly enjoyed working with highly trained professionals where his expertise was appreciated and valued.

Example 4: Claire

Claire grew up in a poor neighborhood. Her single mom took care of her and her younger brother. Claire's father left her mother and younger brother when she was three years old, so she never knew him. Growing up was tough, and there was never enough money. All of the boys she knew were only interested in sports and were "too sloppy," so she didn't date much. She went to a Catholic high school on a scholarship, not because her family was Catholic, but because her mother thought it was an opportunity for her bright daughter to get a better education than she would receive in their neighborhood schools. Claire thrived in the Catholic school environment and excelled in science courses. While most of her friends were out having good times in high school, Claire remained focused on her schoolwork and developed very disciplined study habits. This helped her get a scholastic scholarship to college, where she majored in engineering. She and Dan (mentioned in an earlier example) had a few classes together, even though he was a year behind her. She thought he was driven, and he thought she was a bookworm.

After college, Claire took a job with a small engineering company that seemed to have a bright future. The firm's owner, Bob, was very entrepreneurial and worked on breakthrough designs for clean energy. At first, it was all very exciting, and the money was good. As time drew on, Claire began to become frustrated at the firm, but she couldn't quite figure out why. One day, Bob stopped at her desk to talk with her. There was nothing new in this, as he constantly interacted with the people in his organization. He asked Claire how it was going; Claire replied that it was going okay. Well, "okay" was not what Bob was used to hearing. Most of the people who worked for him were very excited about their jobs, and showed a lot of enthusiasm. With a note of genuine concern, he asked Claire if something was wrong. Claire told him she was consumed by her work, but she never thought it was good enough. As she started talking to Bob, she related to him that the lack of order and procedure in the firm actually made her very uneasy. What the other employees felt as excited fervor for their mission, Claire took as antagonism and chaos. She kept to herself at work, rarely engaging in the heated debates that took place regularly at the firm.

Bob was exceptionally good with people. He knew having the right people on his team meant all the difference if his entrepreneurial venture was going to succeed. Bob realized that even though Claire was very good at her work, the fast paced, hectic atmosphere of a startup business did not fit with her personality. Bob told Claire he really valued her work and contributions to the team, but that he felt she would be a better fit at a more established company. Claire completely agreed with him, although she was afraid this meant Bob was going to fire her. Bob told Claire he had many connections in large corporations, and that she could stay with him for as long as it took to place her with the right company. Claire was relieved that her situation looked like it was going to improve.

Bob helped Claire to get an interview with a Fortune 500 corporation. He gave her a glowing referral, which was largely responsible for her being offered a position. Within a few months at the corporation, Claire knew she had made the right choice. She was relaxed at her new job, and her supervisors were impressed by her diligent, disciplined habits. When she ran into her former classmate, Dan, who told her how frustrated he was at the corporation, she thought he was crazy. Obviously, she and Dan were more different than she realized.

Dan called Claire a month after they had coffee together. Dan had just finished *The Holy Hand Grenade*. He told Claire how much it had done for him and that he realized why the corporation was such a good fit for Claire. He recommended she also read it and take the recommended tests. During their coffee meeting, Claire mentioned that although she really liked working at the corporation, she still didn't know what her life was all about. For some reason, that comment stuck with Dan, and he told her she might find some answers in the book.

Dan was right. Claire read the book, and true to her nature, she diligently followed the recommended procedures. Here is what she found out.

Claire's Personality profile: a C personality, with a Perfectionist pattern.

Claire's goals center on stability with predictable accomplishments. She fears conflict and antagonism from people. Her conscientious attitude and desire to maintain high standards makes her a value to organizations. She is competent, accurate, restrained, and systematic. Her personality likes a clearly defined work environment, and she may not be able to receive compliments very well.

Claire's strength: Discipline

She hates wasting time, so she makes lists and procedures to be efficient. Being on task and on time motivates her. Her world needs to be predictable, ordered, planned, and precise. If she is depressed, it is probably because she made a mistake. She does not like surprises, and she wants to feel in control.

She is an Intrapersonal Thinker

Claire needs solitude to think through issues. She bought a small house with the view of a forest preserve from her home office just to be able to think. The quiet and serenity of her home allow her to find solutions to her problems.

Claire has a significant Father Fracture. Reading *The Holy Hand Grenade* helped her realize how big an effect her father leaving her family when she was three years old has had on her. Even though she developed faith during her Catholic school upbringing, she realized she viewed God as a distant figure who she did not trust to help her in times of need. Recognizing her Father Fracture helped Claire understand why she had trouble really trusting or loving anyone. Now, she had something for her introspective thinking to ponder.

Her love language is quality time. That helps explain why she felt so affirmed when Bob took the time to talk with her about her job at his company. Now Claire knows that "Mister Perfect" will have to want to spend time with her, just doing whatever. She doesn't need gifts or praise, just someone that likes being with her.

After having taken time to contemplate what she had discovered about herself, Claire realized she really did like her job. She decided what she wanted was to be recognized as a leading expert in the corporation. She also acknowledged how alone she felt, and why. The profound effect of being abandoned by her father at age three had distanced her from God, and from any relationship with a man. She finally had the courage to ask her mother what happened. Talking with her mother helped them both to forgive Claire's father and to allow love back into their lives.

Chapter 34

Just Imagine

In between my junior and senior years of college, I was required to attend Marine Corps Officers Candidate School (OCS) as part of my ROTC scholarship. Most of the grueling six-week period spent in Quantico, Virginia was to torture us "candidates" (the word "candidate" implied you were more worthless than whale slime). The drill instructors pushed us to see if we had what it took to be leaders of Marines. Their purpose was to weed out anyone who didn't want badly enough to be a Marine Officer. Some of the training was academic, some was physical, but most of it was psychological. In many ways, it was just like life, but maybe a bit more rigorous.

There were four of us from the University of Virginia (UVA) who went to the same OCS class that summer. Fortunately for us, the UVA Marine ROTC grads who went the year before us told us exactly what to expect. We also had a Marine Staff Sergeant and a Major at UVA whose responsibility it was to prepare us for the rigors of OCS. The fear of not graduating was so high that we probably over-prepared. I made sure I was in the best physical condition of my life before I got there, and the Staff Sergeant and Major coached us on how to get through the psychological mind games they would put us through. What I don't think any of us really prepared for was the academic portion.

The academic parts of OCS were actually pretty easy. The difficult part was staying awake in class. Having little or no sleep, being physically tired all the time, and 95-degree weather with 95 percent humidity and no air conditioning made staying awake a problem for almost everyone. One of my friends from UVA constantly had to stand against a wall instead of sitting in his chair in order to stay awake—but I saw him sleeping while standing up on several occasions. The instructors knew it was a problem, so they helped us a little. Whenever they got to a part of their instruction that was going to be on the test, they would stomp their feet really loudly on the platform, so we would pay attention. It worked well and was greatly appreciated.

Just imagine your life was like my OCS experience. First of all, you are prequalified to go there. In other words, you know you have what it takes to make it through before you even start. Second, you know what you want and are willing to go through some stuff to get it. Third, imagine you knew what to expect before you got there, had people to help prepare you—and they even gave you the test questions and answers ahead of time? What do you think your chances of making it would be?

On the other hand, if you show up at OCS with no training or preparation, making it through could be really doubtful. If you just got on a bus to OCS on a whim, I can guarantee you that the shock of a lifetime would be waiting for you when you stepped of that bus in Quantico. You would have no idea when the torture would end, why you were going through it, or what the rewards would be. Unfortunately, this is the way some of the candidates showed up at OCS, and they didn't last a week. They obviously did not take advantage of the advice of their mentors at their universities, or they did not really want to be there. It was their choice.

You have a choice too.

Just imagine tomorrow morning, rather than stepping off a bus at OCS, you wake up at home to begin your quest. But rather than it just being another day, this day you know who you are. You know what your personality is and how to read the personalities of others. You know how you think, and if you get in a jam, you know what will work for you to think through it. You know how you receive love and give it, so you always feel loved. Most important, you know that your Father approves of you. Your confidence speaks volumes to everyone you meet. Would tomorrow be a different kind of a day if that were true?

Now imagine you know your gift. You know what you are good at, and you know you are better at it than anyone else. You know what your value to the organization is, and your part in accomplishing its vision. Imagine all your self-doubt is gone. You are confident in your ability without being arrogant, and people seek you out for your gift. Just being around you makes other people feel better. You are on a constant learning curve to continually improve your gift, and you absolutely love what you do. Because you are good at what you do, and it is a work of joy, all your money problems are gone or vanishing quickly. Stress in life is at an all time low, and your health is awesome. In fact, you feel better than you have for years and people constantly tell you how great you look. You are on your game, and you know it. Using your gift is what you want to do for the rest of your life.

But wait, it gets better. Imagine you found the cause you want to dedicate yourself to. You found something bigger than yourself that will have an impact on humanity for generations. You found a way to become a part of a legacy. Your gift is needed by this cause. In fact, you know it is vital to the advancement of that cause. You know where you fit in to the big picture. You don't feel the need to compete with others, because the cause is big enough to accommodate everyone's gifts.

So, going back to the beginning, imagine you were King Arthur at the Bridge of Death. However, someone had stomped his feet loudly on a platform (as they did at OCS) the day before, and you knew the questions and the answers before you arrived. How confident would you be to cross that bridge? Imagine you had a mentor to guide you as you continued your quest. Would that help to take some fear out of the unknown? What if you knew this quest was set aside specifically for you by a Father who loved you unconditionally, knowing full well how much joy the quest would bring you before you even started it? Would you be excited to be on the quest?

Imagine your gift helping other people to realize they also have a gift.

Just imagine if even five percent of the people you come into contact with discovered their desires, and they became passionate about what they were doing. Imagine if just five percent of America knew who they were, what they wanted, what their gift was, and were actually engaged in seeking their dream. What problems would that solve? Just imagine!

Of course, you could continue to be aimless and just drift through life. No one would know you made this choice but you. Your Father would still love you; you would still have the same job you have now, and the doubts, stress, and fears you have always had would still be there. Thank God you have the choice.

> For you have not received a spirit of slavery leading to fear again, but you have received a spirit of adoption as sons by which we cry out, "Abba! Father!"

Chapter 35

Epilogue

A MESSAGE FROM YOUR FATHER

My child, I have always known you, and you are my delight. I knew you since before you were born, and I have an awesome, wonderful, even fearfully big plan for you. I have always loved you, and nothing can separate you from my love. Even when you are unlovable, I still love you. Even when you don't love me, I still love you. Even when you hurt your brothers and sisters, I still love you.

I think about you more than you think about yourself, and that is really saying something! You can't hide from me. I see all you do and still love you. When I created you, I did my best work. Oh, how I wish you could see yourself as I see you. You would marvel at the greatness I planted in you. You would wonder how you missed all the gifts I have given you, and how I continue to bless you. There is nothing impossible with me, and I want you to see that I can do far more for you—above anything you could ask for or imagine. That is how big I am, and how much I love you. I just want you to believe me when I tell you this.

You are a one-of-a-kind original. The plan I have for you can only be fulfilled by you. Where you fit in my grand scheme was set aside for you alone. That is how important you are to me. Even if you go off track, I can make all things come back together for your good, but it is your choice. You can choose not to listen to me, and you can choose to go your own way. I will not make you have the abundance I designed for you. If you want to do it all by yourself, be my guest, but beware. Your way will never be as good as my way, and I will not help you do it your way. That is why I have told you to come to me, you who are weary and burdened. I will give you rest. If you do things my way and you learn from me, you will find out how gentle and humble I am. You will have a burden in this life, but my way is easy and my burden is light. Besides, since I own it all anyway, I know what you really want and how you can get it. Regardless of which path you choose, mine or your own, know this: I still love you, and I will always take you back.

When you begin to realize just how much I love you and how many things I have given to you as gifts, you will know I do not ask you to do things for me. My love for you is not conditional on what you do, or don't do. If you choose to show your love for me, it delights me, but it is not a condition of my love and approval of you. I hope you realize I love your brothers and sisters exactly the same as I love you. If you can fathom my love for you, then know that is how much I love those around you. My command to you is to love your brothers and sisters as much as I love you. Even if you don't like them, you should love them because I love them. Even if that is the only reason you love someone else, it is good enough. The way you can demonstrate your love for me is to love what I love.

My child, no matter how old, or how young you are, I hope you can see that your journey has only just begun. I know the plans I have for you; plans for your good and not for calamity. My plans are for your bright future; full of hopes that will be fulfilled. My plans are for an eternity of good things; not just for temporary pleasures.

Knowing who you really are, the gift of greatness I have placed in you, and seeking the desire I gave you will make your journey a delight. It will be full of joy and never grow dull. There is so much more I have for you. I invite you to discover it.

Your loving Father

Recommended Reading

The Holy Bible, God
Before you Quit Your Job, Robert Kiyosaki
Cash Flow Quadrant, Robert Kiyosaki
Deadly Emotions, Dr. Don Colbert
Getting To Know You, Chris Carey
Grown Up Digital, Don Tapscott
Master Key to Riches, Napoleon Hill
Millennials Rising, Neil Howe and William Strauss
Rich Dad Poor Dad, Robert Kiyosaki
StrengthsFinder 2.0, Tom Roth
Succeed and Grow Rich Through Persuasion, Napoleon Hill
The Gift in You, Caroline Leaf
The 5 Love Languages, Gary Chapman
Think and Grow Rich, Napoleon Hill
What Americans Really Want…Really, Frank Luntz
Who Do You Think You Are Anyway, Robert Rohm

About the Author

Thomas J. Gilroy is an author, lecturer, and businessman. He and his wife Mary reside in Foxfire Village, NC. He grew up in Dale City, VA and attended the University of Virginia before being commissioned as a Marine Officer. His military specialty was as an attack helicopter pilot, where he received the nickname of "TJ."

TJ entered the business world after his Marine Corps career, eventually becoming an executive in the tactical equipment industry. He and Mary now own their own research, development, and distribution business, but his passion is working with people to help them discover the seed of greatness within them.

Early in his business career TJ found that asking better questions, resulted in receiving better answers. Whether asking questions of his parents, his Commanding Officers in the Marine Corps, his wife Mary, his mentor Jack, his business associates or friends, or most importantly, the Holy Spirit, the same always held true; ask good questions, get good answers. He also found that the times of his life where he was just drifting, or was really frustrated, were also the times when he stopped asking questions.

Subsequently, his writing style is based on asking questions to help others get the answers to the most important questions in life.

> The anxious longing of the creation waits eagerly for the revealing of the sons of God.
>
> ROMANS 8:19

CPSIA information can be obtained at www.ICGtesting.com
Printed in the USA
LVOW12s1413120913

352015LV00004B/5/P